Windows
XP

QUICK FIX

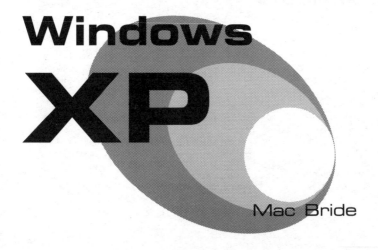

Windows
XP

Mac Bride

QUICK FIX

TEACH YOURSELF BOOKS

For UK orders: please contact Bookpoint Ltd, 130 Milton Park, Abingdon, Oxon OX14 4SB. Telephone: (44) 01235 400414, Fax: (44) 01235 400454. Lines are open 9.00 – 6.00, Monday to Saturday, with a 24-hour message answering service.
You can also order through our website **www.madaboutbooks.com.**

British Library Cataloguing in Publication Data
A catalogue record for this title is available from the British Library.

First published 2002 by Hodder Headline Plc, 338 Euston Road, London, NW1 3BH.

Typeset by Mac Bride, Southampton
Printed in Great Britain for Hodder & Stoughton Educational, a division of Hodder Headline Plc, 338 Euston Road, London NW1 3BH by Cox & Wyman, Reading, Berkshire.

Impression number	10 9 8 7 6 5 4 3 2
Year	2006 2005 2004 2003 2002

Contents

Managing your PC — 151

WINDOWS ESSENTIALS

Getting started

Discover the Desktop

What do you see when you look at the screen? The answer will depend upon what you are doing and how you have set up your PC, but some or all of these items should be visible.

The *background* may be a flat colour, a pattern, a picture or a Web page. It can be changed at any time (see page 108).

Shortcuts are icons with links to programs, to folders (for storing files on the hard disk) or to Web pages. Click an icon to run its program, open the folder or go into the Internet. There are some shortcuts at the start, and you can add your own (see page 98).

The *Taskbar* is normally present as a strip along the bottom of the screen, though it can be moved elsewhere (see page 145). It is the main control centre for the Desktop, carrying the tools and buttons to start and to switch between applications.

Click the **Start** button to open the *Start menu*. Any program on your PC can be run from here. The menu also leads to recently-used documents, favourite places on the Internet, the Help pages and other utilities.

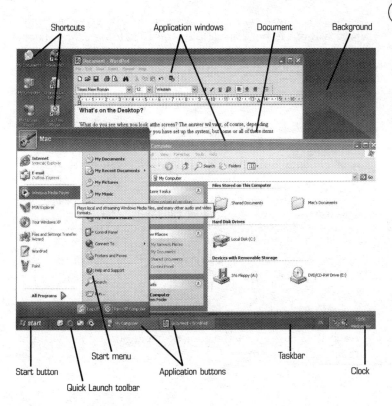

Shortcuts

Application windows

Document

Background

Start button

Quick Launch toolbar

Start menu

Application buttons

Taskbar

Clock

Use the mouse

The mouse is almost essential for work with Windows – you can manage without it, but not as easily. It is used for selecting and manipulating objects, highlighting text, making choices, and clicking icons and buttons – as well as for drawing in graphics applications.

There are five key 'moves'.

Point

Move the mouse so that the tip of the arrow ▷ (or the finger of

the hand 👆) is over the object you want to point to.

- If you point to an icon, and hold the cursor there for a moment, a label will appear, telling you about the icon.

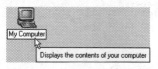

- If you reach the edge of the mouse mat before the pointer has reached its target, pick the mouse up and put it down again in the middle of the mat.

Click

A single click of the left mouse button.

Right-click

A single click of the right mouse button.

Double-click

Two clicks, in quick succession, of the left mouse button. The response of the mouse can be adjusted to suit your double-click speed (see page 126).

Drag

Point to an object or place on the Desktop, hold down the left button and draw the cursor across the screen (see page 33).

Use the keyboard

The keyboard is mainly for entering text, but can also be used for editing text and controlling the system.

These keys are worth identifying and remembering:

Windows – press to open the Start menu. Also used in some keyboard shortcuts.

Control – used in combination with other keys for shortcuts to menu commands.

Alt – mainly used for menu selections (page 10).

Application – displays the shortcut menu (page 12) of the item that is currently selected.

or **Enter** keys, used after entering text or for selecting.

Escape – press this to abandon an operation, e.g. when selecting from a menu or after opening a dialog box by mistake.

The first **Function** key. This one always calls up Help. The others do different jobs, depending upon the application.

⌧	**Tab** – moves a set distance (typically 1cm) across the page in a word-processing program, also moves the cursor from one box to the next in data entry forms.
←	**Backspace** – deletes the selected object on screen or the letter to the left in a block of text.
Delete	**Delete** – deletes the selected object on screen or the letter to the right in a block of text.
Home End	Jump to the top/bottom of a block of text or a window display.
PgUp PgDn	Scroll up/down one window length.
↑ ↓	Move through text, menus and folder displays.
← →	If you hold down **Control** while pressing these, it usually produces faster movement.

Use a menu

The pop-up Start menu and the pull-down menus in Windows applications are structured and used in the same way.

- If an item has an ▸ on the right, a submenu will open when you point to the item.

- If an item has ... after the name, a panel or dialog box (page 15) will open when you point to the item.

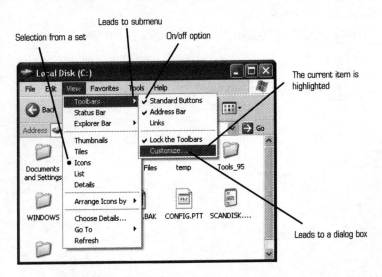

Selection from a set

Leads to submenu

On/off option

The current item is highlighted

Leads to a dialog box

- If an item has ● to its left, it is the selected option from a set.

- If an item has ✔ to its left, it is an option and is turned on – click to turn it off or on again.

- If a name is in grey ('greyed out'), the command is not available at that time – you probably have to select something first.

Select from a menu with the mouse

- To open the Start menu, click on the **Start** button.

- To open a menu in a program, click on its name in the Menu bar.

- To open a submenu, point to its name.

- To run a command or set an option, click on it.

- To leave the menu system without selecting a command, click anywhere else on the screen.

Select from a menu using keys

Open the menu

1 Press the **Windows** button to open the Start menu.

or

2 In a program, hold down **Alt** and press the underlined letter in the name on the Menu bar, e.g. **F** to open the File menu.

Select a command

Either

3 Press the underlined letter of the name to run the command, set the on/off option or open the submenu.

or

4 Move through the menus with the arrow keys – up/down the menu and right to open submenus – then press **Enter**.

◆ The left/right arrows will move you from one menu to the next.

◆ Press **Escape** to close the menu without selecting a command.

Use keyboard shortcuts

Many applications allow you to run some of the most commonly used commands directly from the keyboard, without touching the menu system. For example, in Paint, **Control + S** (i.e. hold down the **Control** key and press **S**) will call up the **Save** command; **Control + O** has the same effect as selecting **Open** from the **File** menu.

The shortcuts vary, and some applications will offer far more than others, but some are common to all – or most – applications. If a command has a keyboard shortcut, it will be shown on the menu, to the right of the name.

Use shortcut menus

Shortcut or *context menus* can be opened for more or less anything on the screen – a Desktop icon, the Taskbar or the background, a file or folder in My Computer, a selected object or block of text in a program. This menu will contain a set of commands and options that are relevant to the object in that context.

To open a shortcut menu

1 Right-click on the object.

or

2 If the object is already selected, press the **Application** key.

3 Select from the menu in the usual way.

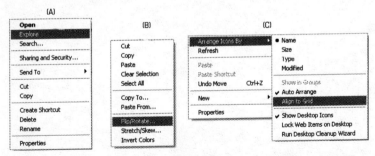

EXAMPLES OF SHORTCUT MENUS, FROM (A) A FOLDER, (B) A SELECTED AREA IN PAINT AND (C) THE DESKTOP

Use the Start menu

The menu has been designed to give you quick access to things that you are likely to need most. On the left are links to recently-used applications, with Internet and e-mail above; on the right are a set of key Windows facilities, and above these are links to folders where you probably keep your documents. If you want an application that isn't listed on the left, click **All Programs**. This opens a menu through which every installed application can be reached (see page 17).

THE START MENU AS IT FIRST APPEARS - YOU
WILL HAVE A DIFFERENT SELECTION OF
APPLICATION LINKS ON THE LEFT.

WINDOWS ESSENTIALS

View properties

Most objects have *Properties*, which define what they look like and how they work. These can be seen and set through the **Properties** panels, which can be reached via the context menus.

Properties panels often have several *tabs*, dealing with different aspects of the object. Some will simply contain information, such as the details of a file; others have options that you can set.

* To switch between tabs, click on the name at the top.

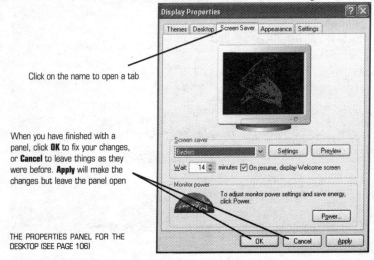

Click on the name to open a tab

When you have finished with a panel, click **OK** to fix your changes, or **Cancel** to leave things as they were before. **Apply** will make the changes but leave the panel open

THE PROPERTIES PANEL FOR THE DESKTOP (SEE PAGE 106)

Set options and properties

An object's options can be set in its Properties panel. Within a program, options are set and information given through *dialog boxes*. The same methods are used in panels and dialog boxes.

Text boxes

File name: Memo.doc

Used for collecting filenames or
other details. Sometimes a value will be suggested by the system.
Edit it, or retype it if necessary.

Click to drop down

Drop-down lists

These look like text boxes but with an
arrow ⌄ to the right. Click on the
arrow to drop down the list, then select
a value.

Power schemes

Home/Office Desk
Home/Office Desk
Portable/Laptop
Presentation
Always On
Minimal Power Management
Max Battery

Lists

With a simple list, just scroll through it and select a value. They sometimes have a linked text box. The selected value is displayed there, but you can also type one in.

Check boxes

These are switches for options – click to turn them on or off. Check boxes are sometimes found singly, but often in sets. You can have any number of check boxes on at the same time, unlike radio buttons.

Radio buttons

These are used to select one from a set of alternatives. Click on the button or its name to select.

Sliders and number values

Click to adjust the value

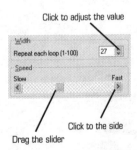

Sliders are used where an approximate value will do – for example, volume control. Drag the slider to increase or decrease, or click to the side of the slider to move it towards the click point.

Numbers are often set through scroll boxes. Click the up or down arrows to adjust the value. If you want to make a big change, type in a new value.

Click to the side

Drag the slider

Start a program

All the programs now on your PC, and any that you install later, should have an entry in the **All Programs** part of the **Start** menu.

A program may be on the first level of this menu, or may have been grouped onto a submenu – which may open up to a further level of submenus. Windows XP sets the basic structure. The installation routines for new software will create the Start menu entries and organize them into submenus, but if you do not like the structure, you can tailor it to suit yourself (see page 146).

To start a program:

1 Click ![start] or press ![key] on your keyboard.

2 Point to **All Programs** with the mouse.

3 If the program name is not visible, point to a group name to open the next level of menu – and again if necessary.

4 Click once on a program name.

tip

The programs that you have used most recently are listed on the left of the Start menu.

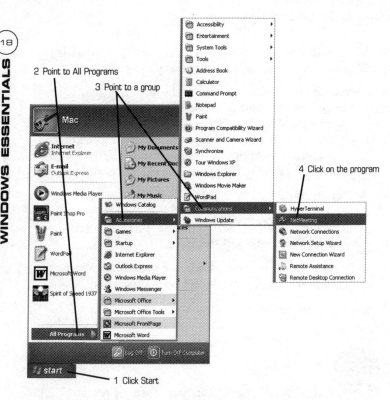

2 Point to All Programs

3 Point to a group

4 Click on the program

1 Click Start

RUNNING A PROGRAM FROM THE START MENU. IN THIS CASE, THE PROGRAM, **NETMEETING**, IS ON THE SECOND LEVEL OF SUBMENUS

Start from Documents

The documents that you have worked on recently can be opened from the My Recent Documents folder on the Start menu.

1 Click on **Start**.

2 Point to **My Recent Documents** to open a list of documents.

3 Select a document to run the linked application and open the document.

tip

Documents can also be opened from My Computer (page 62).

Start from the Desktop

Shortcuts offer a quick route to folders and programs. When you first start using Windows XP, you will find a dozen of these icons on the Desktop. Some, such as My Documents, lead to folders – click on these and My Computer will run, open at the selected folder. Others, such as the Internet Explorer icon, lead to applications – click on these to start the application.

If you want to add shortcuts to favourite applications, it can be done easily through My Computer (see page 98).

tip

Every document type is linked to an application (see page 70, *Understand file types*), so that when you open a document, Windows will run the appropriate application for you.

Start from the Quick Launch toolbar

The Quick Launch toolbar gives you ready access to three commonly used applications: Internet Explorer, Outlook Express and Media Player.

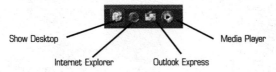

Show Desktop

Internet Explorer   Outlook Express

Media Player

• Click the Show Desktop icon to hide any open windows so that you can see the Desktop.

• Click it again to restore all the hidden windows to view.

You can add shortcuts to the toolbar or create new Taskbar toolbars (see page 142).

tip

See *Quick Fix Internet Explorer 5.5/Outlook Express 5* for more on these Internet applications.

Turn Off

When you have finished a working session, you must shut down the system properly.

1 Click **Start** and select **Turn Off Computer**. If any windows are open, they will be closed. You may be prompted to save documents.

2 Select **Turn Off**.

Restart will normally restore order after a crash – see page 24

tip

Some PCs have a Stand By or Suspend mode which shuts down the screen and hard drive, but leaves the memory intact, allowing a very quick startup when you next want to use the PC.

Log Off

If you are on a network or there are several user accounts on the
PC, you should log off at the end of a session. Select **Log Off** on
the Start menu and then...

◆ Click **Log Off** at the prompt. This shuts any open programs,
  but leaves the PC on, for you or another user to use later.

or

◆ Click **Switch User** at the prompt. This suspends your programs and allows another user to log in. It doesn't matter if
  they use the same programs as you have been using – the
  documents that you were working on will not (normally) be
  affected by anything they do. When they are finished you can
  log in again and pick up where you left off.

SELECT **SWITCH USER** TO LEAVE YOUR PROGRAMS SUSPENDED WHILE SOMEONE ELSE USES THE MACHINE, OR
LOG OFF IF YOU HAVE DONE FOR THE DAY.

Recover from a crash

Windows XP is quite robust, but software is rarely perfect. Some applications – and some combinations of applications – are more likely than others to crash.

You will know your system has crashed if:

- The busy symbol ⧖ appears and stays (but do wait twice as long as normal just in case it has a lot more to do than you thought).

- There is no response to key presses or mouse actions.

tip

Crashes are normally caused by two programs trying to use the same area of memory, and you can go find a big technical book if you want to know more about this!

Solution

1 Hold down **Ctrl** and **Alt**, and press **Delete**. The **Windows Task Manager** dialog box will appear.

2 The programs listed on the **Applications** tab should all have *Running* Status. If one is not running, select it and click **End Task** – you will be asked to confirm that you really want to close it. The system should work properly once it is out of the way.

If the program that is giving you problems is marked **Running**, it probably hasn't crashed – close the Task Manager and give Windows a bit longer to sort itself out

Some crashes won't respond to this. In these cases, just turn the PC off.

Basic techniques

Select text

Before you can do any work on an object – e.g. format a block of text, copy part of an image, move a group of files from one folder to another – you must select it.

Select text with the mouse:

1 Point to the start of the text.

2 Hold down the left mouse button and drag the cursor over the screen.

3 The selected text will be highlighted.

Select text with the keyboard:

1 Move the cursor to the start of the text.

2 Hold down the **Shift** key.

3 Use **Home**, **End**, **Page Up**, **Page Down** or the arrow keys to highlight the text you want.

MOUSE
Drag over the area, holding the left button down

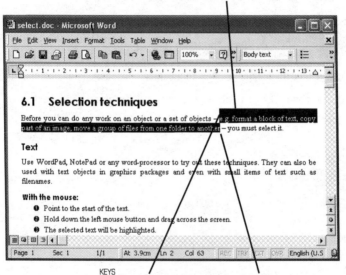

6.1 Selection techniques

Before you can do any work on an object or a set of objects – e.g. format a block of text, copy part of an image, move a group of files from one folder to another – you must select it.

Text

Use WordPad, NotePad or any word-processor to try out these techniques. They can also be used with text objects in graphics packages and even with small items of text such as filenames.

With the mouse:

❶ Point to the start of the text.

❷ Hold down the left mouse button and drag across the screen.

❸ The selected text will be highlighted.

KEYS
Point to the start, hold down **Shift** and move to the end

Select graphics or icons

Single object:

♦ Point to it. If this does not highlight it, click on it.

Adjacent objects:

1 Imagine a rectangle that will enclose the objects.

2 Point to one corner of this rectangle.

3 Hold down the left mouse button and drag across to the opposite corner – an outline will appear as you do this.

Point to one corner

Drag to the opposite corner

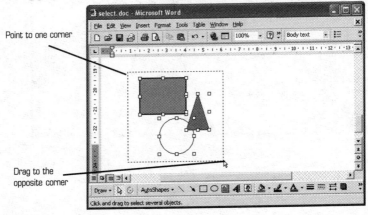

or

4 Select the object at one corner.

5 Hold down **Shift** and select the object at the opposite corner.

Select the first object

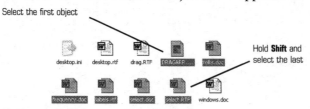

Hold **Shift** and
select the last

Scattered objects:

1 Highlight the first object.

2 Hold down the **Ctrl** key and highlight each object in turn.

3 If you select an object by mistake, point to (or click on) it
   again to remove the highlighting.

Select the first object

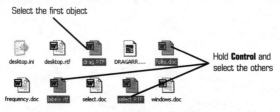

Hold **Control** and
select the others

Delete objects or text

The same techniques are used on the Desktop and in programs, and apply to objects and to characters or blocks of text.

1 Select the object(s) or block of text.

2 Right-click for the shortcut menu or – in a program – open the **Edit** menu and select **Delete**.

or

3 Press the **Delete** or **Backspace** key.

tip

If you delete something by mistake, you can usually recover it either by pressing **Control + Z** or with the **Undo** command on the **Edit** menu.

Cut, Copy and Paste

These can copy and move data within and between applications.

- **Copy** copies a selected block of text, picture, file or other object into a special part of memory called the *Clipboard*.

- **Cut** deletes the data, but places a copy into the Clipboard.

- **Paste** inserts the data into a new place in the same or a different application.

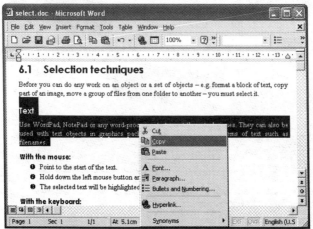

THE SHORT MENU OFFERS THE QUICKEST ROUTE TO THE CUT AND PASTE COMMANDS. IF THE CLIPBOARD IS EMPTY, PASTE WILL BE 'GREYED OUT' OR OMITTED FROM THE MENU

Selected graphics usually have an enclosing frame with 'handles' at the corners and mid-sides. You can drag within the frame to move the object, or on the handles to resize it

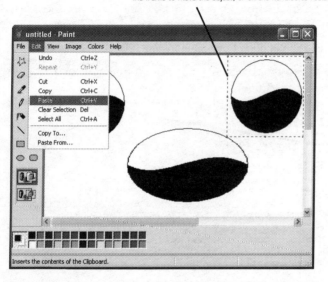

PASTING A COPIED IMAGE IN PAINT – THE SAME DATA CAN BE COPIED AS MANY TIMES AS YOU WANT – AND IN THE SAME OR IN DIFFERENT APPLICATIONS

Drag and drop

Use this for moving objects within or between applications, or for rearranging files and folders (see page 78).

1 Select the block of text or the object(s).

2 Click anywhere within the highlighted text or object, then hold down the mouse button and drag the object across the screen or, with text, move the cursor (which is now $\aleph$).

3 Release the button to drop the object into its new position.

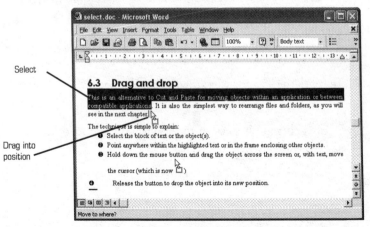

Select

Drag into position

DRAGGING TEXT IN WORDPAD. THE TARGET POSITION IS MARKED BY THE LINE TO THE LEFT OF THE ARROW

Use scraps

A 'scrap' is a special sort of file parked on the Desktop. It is typically a fragment of a word-processor document – though it could be the whole of one. Scraps can be used as highly visible reminders of urgent jobs, or to hold blocks of text that you will reuse in other files, or simply as temporary storage.

What distinguishes a scrap from an ordinary file are the ways that it is created and used.

1 Set the word-processor window into Restore mode (page 52) so that some of the Desktop is visible.

2 Select the text.

3 Drag the selection and drop it on the Desktop.

4 To reuse the scrap, either drag it into the application window,

or

5 Double-click on it to open the application and load in the scrap document.

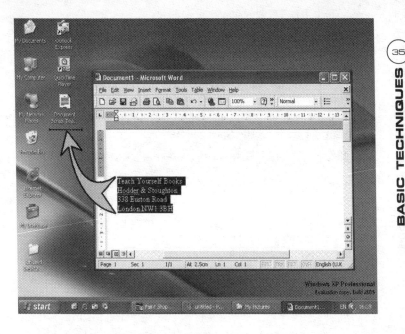

CREATING A SCRAP. TO REUSE IT, DRAG IT BACK INTO THE APPLICATION.

Help

Get Help and Support

The main Windows XP Help system is reached through the **Help and Support** item on the **Start** menu.

• Click **Start**, select **Help and Support** and you are in.

The Home page

On the left of the Home page is a set of major topic headings. Each of these leads to a contents list for the topic, and here you will find three types of links.

▢ beside a heading shows that this will open a list of sub-topic links in the right pane – and clicking one of these will display a page of Help.

⊞ indicates a group of headings – click to reveal the ▢ headings.

▣ is used for *See also* links, to the glossary, list of keyboard shortcuts list, tools and related newsgroups (discussion groups on the Internet).

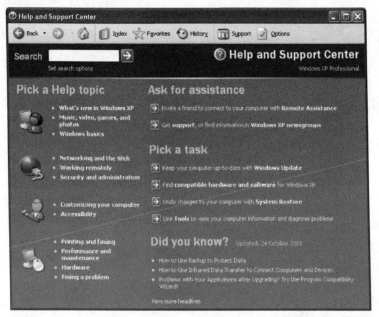

tip

You can also start Windows Help and Support from the Desktop, or get Help within any application, by pressing [F1].

WINDOWS ESSENTIALS

Click for a list of links to Help pages on that topic

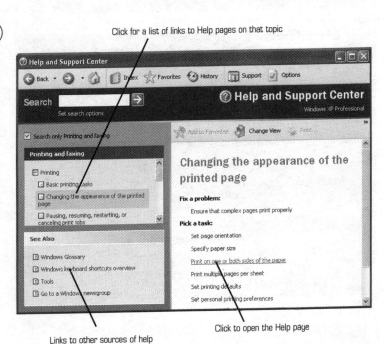

Links to other sources of help

Click to open the Help page

PICKING A HELP TOPIC AT THE HOME PAGE OF HELP AND SUPPORT OPENS A LIST OF HEADINGS, EACH OF WHICH LEADS TO A LIST OF SUB-TOPIC LINKS – CLICK ON THESE TO DISPLAY THEIR HELP PAGES.

Use a troubleshooter

The troubleshooters will take you through a series of checks and activities to try to diagnose and cure problems.

1 Work through the contents to find a relevant topic.
2 If there is a troubleshooter listed at the bottom, click on it.
3 Follow the instructions – and they usually work!

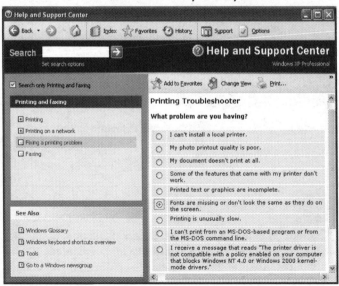

Find Help through the Index

To switch to the Index:

1 Click on the Index label in the menu bar.

2 Drag on the slider or click the down arrow to scroll through the Index entries.

or

3 Start to type a keyword in the top box. As you type, the list will scroll to the words that begin with the typed letters.

4 Pick a topic from the list and click [Display].

5 If there are several Help pages for the same index entry, you will be offered a choice – pick one and click [Display].

The Help pages that you find here are the same as those linked from the Home page.

tip

A 'keyword' is simply a word that describes what it is you are looking for. If a word does not give you what you want, try a different word to describe it.

If you start to type, the list scrolls to those letters

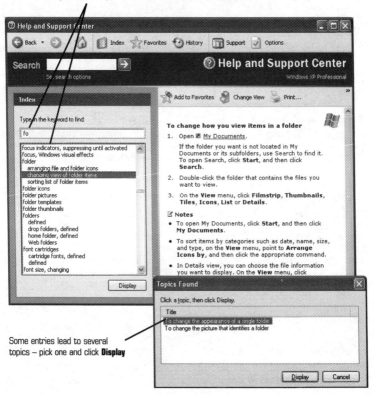

Some entries lead to several
topics – pick one and click **Display**

Search for Help

The **Search** box is present on every page of the Help system.

1 To run a search, type your keyword into the box and click ⬛.

2 The results are grouped in three sets – click the headers to see their results:

+ **Suggested Topics** are normally the most useful. These are the pages that have been indexed by the keyword;

+ **Full-text Search Matches** are pages which contain your keywords, but these may only be passing references;

+ **Microsoft Knowledge Base** draws help from Microsoft's Web site and is, of course, only available if you are online.

Type a keyword and click the arrow

Click on the header bar to open a group

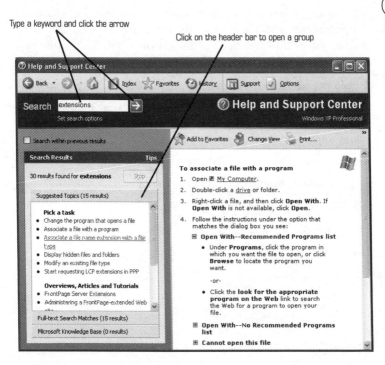

Change the Help View

The **Change View** option shuts down the surrounding Help and Support window and leaves just the topic display. This can be very useful if you want to keep the information visible while you tackle that tricky job.

1 On the header bar of the Help topic, click **Change View**.

2 If necessary, resize the window and move it to a convenient part of the screen so that you can still read it while working on whatever you needed the Help on.

♦ Click **Change View** to reopen the full window when needed.

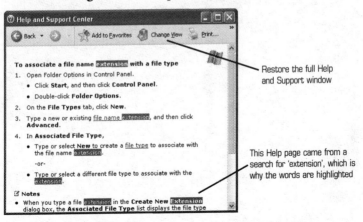

Restore the full Help and Support window

This Help page came from a search for 'extension', which is why the words are highlighted

Online support

The Help system offers three types of online support, and none of them are for the faint-hearted.

* **Ask a friend to help** will let you connect to a friend through the Internet Messenger system (if you have suitable friends who use this and also have XP). You can then talk about your problem with your friend, who can view your screen and even operate your PC through the Internet. That's the theory. Drop me an e-mail (at *macbride@tcp.co.uk*) if you've tried it!

* **Get help from Microsoft** takes you to their technical support area on the Web. This is very useful service for the technically minded but can be heavy going for the rest of us.

* **Go to a Windows Web site forum** links to the newsgroups where XP is discussed. These can be useful resources, particularly for the more experienced user, but even new users may get some help here.

It takes longer to get Help online, but there is far more available over a far wider range of topics.

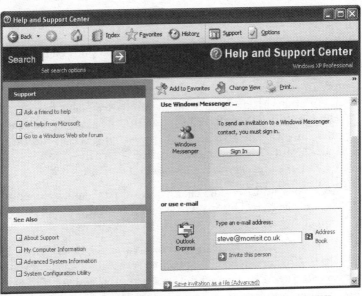

YOU CAN ASK A FRIEND TO HELP – IF YOU HAVE ONE WHO IS WILLING AND ABLE AND USES MESSENGER.

tip

If you read to the bottom of a Help page, you will normally see the label 'Related topics'. Click on this to open a list of links to other pages on similar topics.

USING WINDOWS

Managing windows

Identify the parts

A window is a framed area of the screen that exists independently of any other windows. All applications are displayed in windows. If an application can handle multiple documents, each document is displayed in its own window within the application.

All windows have these features:

* **Title bar** along the top – showing the name of the application or document;

* **Minimize, Maximize/Restore** and **Close** buttons on the far right of the title bar – for changing the mode (page 52) and for shutting down;

* An icon at the far left of the Title Bar – leading to the window's **Control menu** (page 53);

* **Scroll bars** along the right and bottom – for moving the contents within the frame. These are only present if the contents are too wide or too long to fit within the frame.

* A thin outer **border** – for changing the size (see page 56).

Control menu

Title bar

Menu bar

Toolbars

Minimize

Maximize/Restore

Close

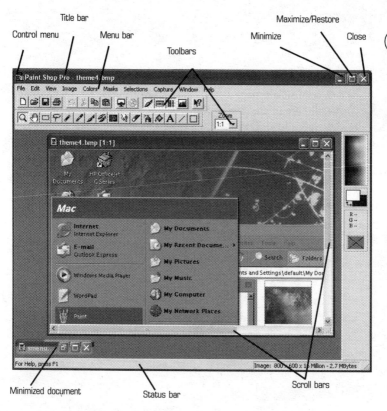

Minimized document

Status bar

Scroll bars

Application windows also have:

+ **Menu bar** – giving access to the full range of commands and options;

+ One or more **Toolbars** – containing icons that call up the more commonly used commands and options. Toolbars are normally along the top of the working area, but may be down either side, or as 'floating' panels anywhere on screen.

+ The **Status bar** – displaying a variety of information about the current activity in the application.

Scroll through the window

If a document is too wide or too long to fit within the window, scroll bars will be present along the bottom and/or right of the frame. These can be used to move the hidden parts of the document into the working area.

* Click on the arrows at the ends to nudge the contents slowly in the direction of the arrow.

* Click on the bar to the side of or above or below the slider to move in larger jumps.

* Drag the slider. This is the quickest way to scroll through a large document.

Small movement   Large movement   Slider – drag as needed

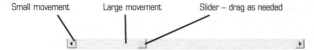

tip

If the typing, drawing or other movements that you make while working on your document take the current position out of the visible area, the document will be scrolled automatically to bring the current position back into view.

Minimize, Maximize and Restore

A window can be in one of three modes.

Switch between them with the buttons at the top right:

Maximize – An application window fills the screen and loses its outer frame. When a document window is maximized, its Title bar is merged with the application Title bar.

Restore – The window is smaller than the full screen or working area. Its size can be adjusted, and it can be moved to any position – within or beyond the limits of the screen.

Minimize – A minimized application becomes a button on the Taskbar. A minimized document shows only the Title bar and window control buttons.

Controlling windows with keys

The Control menu allows you to change the window mode with keystrokes.

1 Press **Alt** and **Space bar** to open the menu in applications.

2 Press **Alt** and the **Minus** key to open the menu for a document.

3 Press the keys of the underlined letters to **Mi<u>n</u>imize, Ma<u>x</u>imize/<u>R</u>estore** or **<u>C</u>lose**. (Or press **Alt + F4** to close.)

♦ You can also start to **<u>M</u>ove** (page 58) or change the **<u>S</u>ize** (page 57) of the window from here.

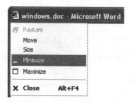

tip

The Control menu can be opened by clicking the icon at the far left of the Title bar, but if you are using the mouse it makes more sense to click the control buttons on the right.

Switch between windows

You can have any number of windows – each running its own program – open at once. You can only ever work on one application at a time – though you can copy or move data between two windows and there may be continuing activities, such as printing, going on in other windows. If you do not need to see what is happening in the other windows, the simplest layout is to run all applications in Maximized mode. The one that you are working on will fill the screen, obscuring the others.

To bring a window to the front:

♦ Click its button on the Taskbar.

or

1 Hold down the **Windows** key and press **Tab**. This will select the first Taskbar button – press **Tab** again to move to the next.

2 When the one you want is selected, press **Enter** to open its window.

View multiple windows

If you want to see two or more windows at the same time –
perhaps to copy material from one to another – the simplest way
is to use the **Cascade** or **Tile** commands. They take the windows
currently open in Maximized or Restore mode and arrange them
overlapping (**Cascade**), side-by-side (**Tile Horizontally**) or one
above the other (**Tile Vertically**).

1 Right-click on a blank area of the Taskbar.

2 Select **Cascade** or **Tile Horizontally/Vertically**.

To return to the previous layout:

3 Right-click the Taskbar again. The menu will now have an
   Undo Cascade or **Undo Tile** command.

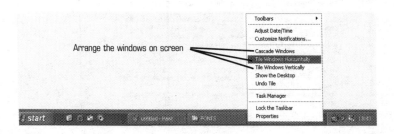

Arrange the windows on screen

Resize a window with the mouse

When a window is in Restore mode, its size can be adjusted.

1 Point to an edge or corner of the frame – when you are in a suitable place the cursor changes to a double-headed arrow.

2 Hold down the left button and drag the edge or corner to change the window size.

3 Release the mouse button.

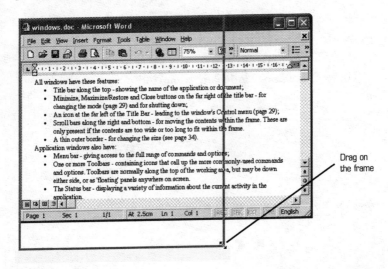

Drag on the frame

Resize with the keyboard

1 Open the Control menu (see page 53).

2 Press **S** to select Size.

3 Press the arrow key corresponding to the edge that you want to move. A double-headed arrow will appear on that edge.

4 Use the arrow keys to move the edge into its new position.

5 Press **Enter** to fix the new size.

tip

If you have turned on the **Show windows contents while dragging** option (on the **Effects** tab of the **Display Properties**, see page 116), the window will change size as you drag or press the arrow keys. If the option is off, you will see a shaded outline showing the new window size.

Move a window

A window in Restore mode can be moved to anywhere on – or part-ways off – the screen (or the working area in an application).

Moving with the mouse

◆ Point to anywhere on the Title bar and drag the window into its new place.

Moving with the keyboard

1 Open the Control menu and select **Move**.

2 Use the arrow keys to move the window as required.

3 Press **Enter** to fix the new position.

Close a window

When you have finished with a window, close it. This will free up memory so that other applications run more smoothly, as well as reducing the clutter on your Desktop.

There are three methods which will work with any window:

- Click the **Close** button ☒ in the top right corner.
- Hold down the **Alt** key and press **F4**.
- Exit from the application – usually with **Exit** or **Close** on the **File** menu.

Managing files

Files and folders

A typical hard drive has 20 Gigabytes of storage, and this must be organized if you are ever to find anything. The organization comes through *folders*. A folder is an elastic-sided division of the disk. It can contain any number of files and subfolders – which can contain other subfolders. At the simplest, a C: drive might contain three folders – *My Documents*, *Program Files* and *Windows* – with each of these having subfolders for different sets of files or programs. You can create new folders, rename, delete or move them to produce your own folder structure.

Understand filenames

Every document's filename has two parts.

The first part of the name can be more or less anything you want and as long as you like (up to 250 characters!). It can consist of any combination of letters, numbers, spaces and underlines, but no other symbols. The name should be meaningful, so that you can easily identify the file when you come back to it later.

The second part is a three-letter extension which identifies the type of document. This is normally set by the application in which it was created, and it is through this extension that Windows can link documents and applications (see page 70).

Some common extensions:

.TXT	Simple text, e.g. from NotePad
.DOC	Word document
.HTM	Web page
.BMP	bitmap images, e.g. from Paint
.GIF	a standard format for image on Web pages
.JPG	an alternative format for Web page images
.WAV	audio file in Wave format
.EXE	an executable program – not a document!

Open My Computer

My Computer, Windows Explorer and Internet Explorer are all aspects of the same program, with slightly different displays and selections of tools. You can change any one into the other. Type an Internet address into My Computer or Windows Explorer and it will become Internet Explorer. Start to browse your hard disk from Internet Explorer and it will become Windows Explorer.

My Computer is started from the Desktop icon. It is Windows Explorer at its simplest, with the display set to just show the contents of one drive or folder.

If you set My Computer so that it opens a new window for every folder (one of the Folder Options, see page 66), it can also be used for reorganizing your file storage.

Common Tasks

Click to display folders in the
Explorer Bar (see page 64)

Click on a disk or folder
to display its contents

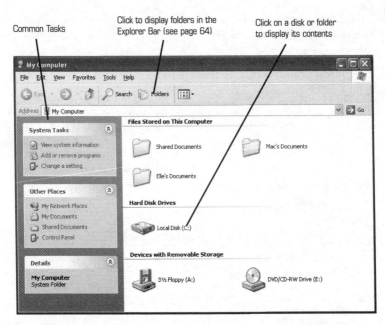

MY COMPUTER, AS IT FIRST APPEARS, WITH LARGE ICONS, AND COMMON TASKS OPEN ON THE LEFT

Explore your folders

You can manage your files and folders much better if you display the *Folders* in the Explorer Bar (which turns My Computer into Windows Explorer).

1 Click 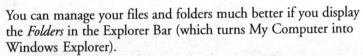 to display Folders in the Explorer Bar.

2 In the folder display, ⊞ to the left of a folder name shows that it has subfolders. Click this to open up the branch. The icon changes to ⊟ – click this to close the branch.

When a folder is selected 📁, its files and subfolders are listed in the main pane. Files can be listed by name, type, date or size, and displayed as thumbnails or large or small icons, with or without details (see page 73).

The **Status bar** at the bottom shows the number of objects in the folder and the amount of memory they use, or the size of a selected file. If the **Status Bar** is not visible, it can be turned on from the View menu.

tip

If you run Windows Explorer (on the Accessories menu), it opens with the Explorer Bar turned on.

Open a folder to display its subfolders

Select a folder to display its contents

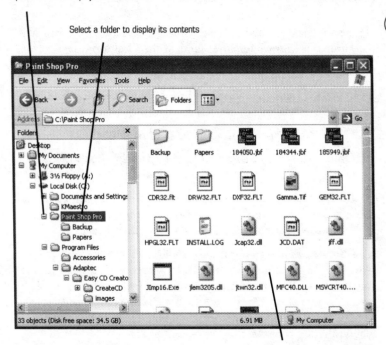

The files are shown here in **Icons View** – see page 73 for more on Views

WITH THE FOLDER LIST DISPLAYED, MY COMPUTER BECOMES WINDOWS EXPLORER

Set your Folder Options

This panel lets you control the behaviour and appearance of My Computer/Windows Explorer (and of the Desktop).

+ To reach it, open the **Tools** menu and select **Folder Options**.

In the **Click items...** section, set how you want the computer to respond to single and double-clicks. I would recommend:

+ **Open with a single click** if you are a new user – it's simpler.

+ **Double-click to open** if you have previously used earlier versions of Windows – it's the familiar way of working.

In the **Tasks** area, **Show common tasks in folders** will give you a 'richer' experience, with decorated folders and previews of files. Use **Windows classic folders** for a simpler file display.

The **Browse Folders** option only applies when the Explorer Bar is turned off. **Open each folder in its own window** is useful for moving files from one to another, but can produce a cluttered screen. If you select **Open each folder in the same window**, you can make it open in a new window if you hold down **Control** when opening the folder.

+ When you have set the options, click **OK** to close the panel.

The **common tasks** display makes some jobs easier, but the **classic folders** gives you a clearer overview of your system, its drives and folders

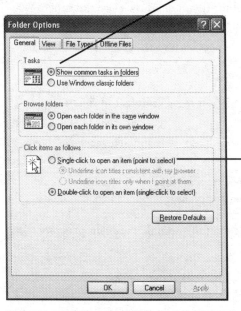

Whichever **Click items...** option you set, you can make My Computer do the reverse by holding down **Control** when you open the folder

THE GENERAL OPTIONS SET TO SHOW COMMON TASKS AS THE DEFAULT

Set your folder views

Click **Like Current Folder** if you want its View and other settings to be applied to all folders.

Click **Reset All Folders** to go back to the original settings.

Advanced Settings

Most of these should be left at their defaults but note these:

Hidden files – Windows XP 'hides' essential files and (crucial) system files, to prevent accidental deletion. They can be shown if you do want to see them.

Remember each folder's view settings will retain the separate options from one session to the next. The settings can be different for each folder, for example you may want more detail in folders that contain documents than in those that contain program files.

Windows only hides files if they are essential, and if they are hidden, they cannot be moved or deleted by accident!

If a file is **registered** (see page 70) the Type column shows its associated program, so the extension serves less purpose – almost all file types *are* known

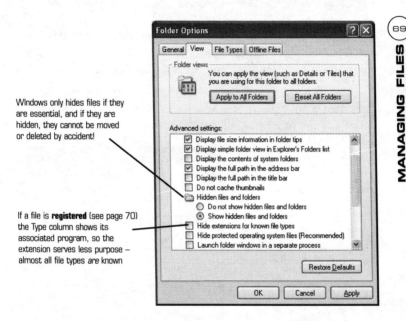

Folder Options ? ✕

General | View | File Types | Offline Files

Folder views

You can apply the view (such as Details or Tiles) that you are using for this folder to all folders.

[Apply to All Folders]   [Reset All Folders]

Advanced settings:

- ☑ Display file size information in folder tips
- ☑ Display simple folder view in Explorer's Folders list
- ☐ Display the contents of system folders
- ☑ Display the full path in the address bar
- ☐ Display the full path in the title bar
- ☐ Do not cache thumbnails
- 📁 Hidden files and folders
  - ○ Do not show hidden files and folders
  - ⦿ Show hidden files and folders
- ☐ Hide extensions for known file types
- ☐ Hide protected operating system files (Recommended)
- ☐ Launch folder windows in a separate process

[Restore Defaults]

[OK]   [Cancel]   [Apply]

Understand file types

Documents can be associated with applications, so that picking one from the **Documents** list on the **Start** menu or from a folder will start up its application and open the document within it.

The **File Types** tab lists all the 'registered' file types – the ones associated with applications. Select one from the list, and in the bottom of the panel you will see the application that the document **Opens with**.

To change the settings for the selected extension, click **Change** and give the new details at the dialog box

Several extensions may be associated with one application – use the **Advanced** button to change the settings for them all

Folder Options   ? ☒

General | View | File Types | Offline Files

Registered file types:

Extensions	File Types
CSS	Cascading Style Sheet Document
CSV	Microsoft Excel Comma Separated Values File
CUR	Cursor
CUT	Paint Shop Pro Image
DB	Data Base File
DER	Security Certificate
DESK	DESKLINK File

New   Delete

Details for 'CSV' extension

Opens with: ▨ Microsoft Excel for Window   Change...

Files with extension 'CSV' are of type 'Microsoft Excel Comma Separated Values File'. To change settings that affect all 'Microsoft Excel Comma Separated Values File' files, click Advanced.

Advanced

OK   Cancel   Apply

Associate file types

If a program's installation routine doesn't set up the association, you can do it yourself. It can be done via the **New** button on the **File Types** tab, but this method is easier. Close the **Folder Options** panel.

1 Later, when you try to open a document of an unregistered type, you will be presented with the **Open With** panel.

2 Select an application – if it is not listed, but you know that it is on your PC, click **Browse...** and track down the program's .EXE file.

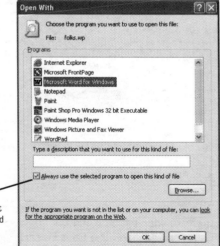

3 If you want to give a description (to appear in the **File Types** list), do so.

4 Click **OK**.

If you do not want to set up a permanent link with an application, clear this box and the document will be opened with the chosen program on this occasion only

The tools

- **Back** and **Forward** move between the last folders that you have opened.

- **Up** takes you up to the next level folder.

- **Search** starts the Search facility (page 92) in the Explorer bar.

- **Folder** displays the Folder List in the Explorer bar.

- **Views** drops down a list of the main View options.

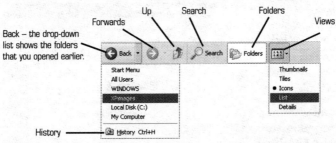

Back – the drop-down list shows the folders that you opened earlier.

Up

Forwards

Search

Folders

Views

History

HISTORY (AND, TO A LESSER EXTENT, **SEARCH**) ARE MAINLY USED WHEN EXPLORING THE INTERNET

tip

There are buttons for most commands. If you want to add them to your toolbar, use the **View → Toolbars → Customize** command to open the Customize Toolbar dialog box.

Set your View options

Files and folders can be shown in various ways:

* *Filmstrip* shows thumbnails of the pictures, with a larger preview of the selected picture above.

* *Thumbnails* shows – if possible – a miniature image of each file. It is, of course, best for use with images, but it can be handy for Web pages and some formatted documents.

* *Tiles* displays for each file a large icon (so it is easy to identify the type), plus details of its type, size, date and author (if appropriate).

* *Icons* and *List* differ mainly in the size of the icons and in the order – icons has slightly larger images and lists across the screen. Both are good for selecting sets of files (see page 92).

* *Details* gives a column display under the headings Name, Size, Type and Modified. Click on a heading to sort the files in ascending order by that feature. Click a second time to sort them in descending order. This display is useful for tracking down files that you were working on at a certain date (but have forgotten the names), or for finding old or large files if you need to create some space.

Set the style from the **View** menu or the **View** drop-down list.

USING WINDOWS

FILMSTRIP VIEW (TOP) IS A GOOD WAY TO BROWSE THROUGH A FOLDER OF PICTURES. **THUMBNAILS VIEW** IS EXCELLENT FOR FINDING IMAGES AND SOME TYPES OF FORMATTED FILES – BUT YOU DON'T GET MANY TO A SCREENFUL.

TILES VIEW (TOP) HAS EASY-TO-SEE ICONS AND TELLS YOU THE KEY DETAILS ABOUT EACH FILE. **ICONS VIEW** DISPLAYS A LOT OF FILES ONTO THE SCREEN – **LIST VIEW** PACKS EVEN MORE ON – BUT YOU CAN SEE THE DETAILS OF ANY CHOSEN FILE IF YOU HAVE COMMON TASKS IN THE EXPLORER BAR.

Sort files into order

In Details View you can sort the files into ascending or descending order by name, size, type or date.

1 Open the **View** menu or the **View** drop-down list and select **Details**.

2 Click on a column heading to sort the files in ascending order by that feature.

3 Click a second time on the same heading to sort them in descending order.

tip

When you want to tidy up an over-filled folder, sort it by date or type to group together sets of files for moving or deleting.

Click on the heading to sort – the arrow
shows the direction of the sort order

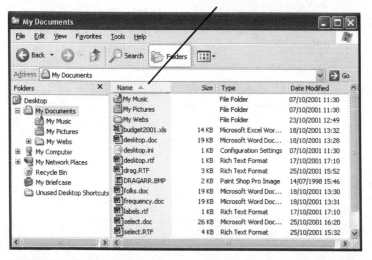

IF THERE ARE A LOT OF FILES IN A FOLDER, SORTING THEM IN DETAILS VIEW WILL OFTEN HELP YOU TO LOCATE THE
ONES YOU WANT. NOTE THAT WHEN YOU SORT A FOLDER BY NAME, FOLDERS ARE LISTED FIRST BEFORE FILES.

Organize your folders

Windows XP sets up one folder for your files, called *My Documents*. This is unlikely to be enough for very long. You need to create more folders if:

◆ you will be storing more than a few dozen documents – it's hard to find stuff in crowded folders;

◆ more than one person uses the PC – everyone should have their own storage space;

◆ your documents fall into distinct categories – personal, hobbies, different areas of work, etc.

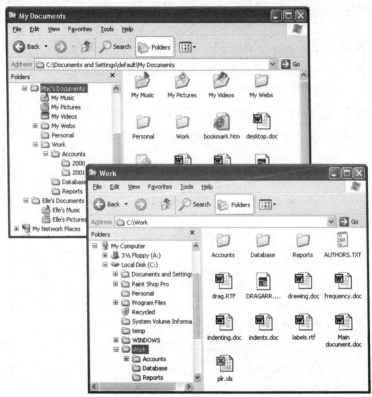

TWO APPROACHES TO A FOLDER STRUCTURE: IN THE TOP ONE, THE NEW FOLDERS HAVE BEEN CREATED WITHIN *MY DOCUMENTS*; IN THE LOWER, THE FOLDERS ARE ALL AT THE MAIN LEVEL. EITHER WORKS JUST AS WELL

Create a folder

A new folder can be created at any point in the folder structure.

1 In the Folder list in the Explorer Bar, select the folder which will contain the new one.

2 Open the **File** menu, point to **New** then select **Folder**.

3 Replace *New Folder* with a meaningful name.

Use File → New → Folder

Where will it go?

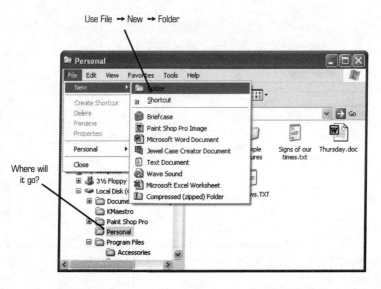

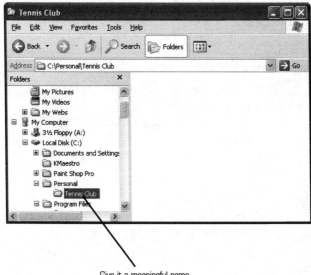

Give it a meaningful name

tip

If you decide the folder is in the wrong place, select it and drag it into place in the Folders list.

Move files to another folder

Click **Folders** to display the folder list in the Explorer Bar.

1 Select the file(s).

2 Scroll through the folder display and/or open subfolders, if necessary, until you can see the target folder.

3 Drag the file(s) across the screen until the target folder is highlighted, then drop it there.

If you can't remember how to select several items at once, see *Select graphics or icons*, page 28.

USING WINDOWS

tip

Files are only copied if the target is on the same disk. If it is on another disk, the files are moved.

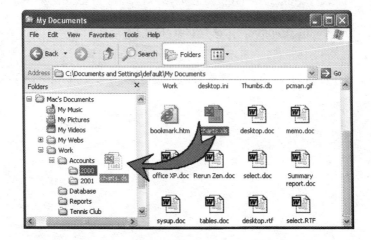

IF YOU CAN SEE THE TARGET FOLDER, YOU CAN DRAG FILES INTO IT

Copy files to a floppy

Click **Folders** to display the folder list in the Explorer Bar.

1 Place a formatted disk (see page 183) in the A: drive.

2 Select the file(s).

3 Scroll through the Folder display until you can see the A: drive and drag the file(s) across the screen until the A: drive icon is highlighted, then drop it there.

or

4 Right-click on the file and select **Send to → 3½ Floppy (A:)**

Copy files on the same disk

Click **Folders** to display the folder list in the Explorer Bar.

1 Select the file(s).

2 Set the Folder display so that you can see the target folder.

3 Hold down the right mouse button and drag the file(s) onto the target folder.

4 Release the button. A shortcut menu appears.

5 Select **Copy Here**.

◆ The file will be named *Copy of...* followed by its original name. Edit this if required.

To *move* a file from one disk to another, hold down the right mouse button while you drag. When you drop the file, select **Move Here** from the short menu.

Copy To or Move To Folder

A slower, but more reliable alternative to drag and drop is to use the **Copy To** and **Move To Folder** commands.

1 Select the file(s).

2 To move a file, open the **Edit** menu and select **Move to Folder...**

3 To copy, open the **Edit** menu and select **Copy to Folder...**

4 The **Browse For Folder** dialog box will open. Work your way down through the folder structure and select the target folder, then click **OK**.

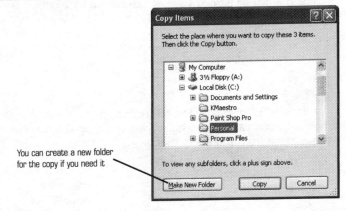

Copy Items   [?][X]

Select the place where you want to copy these 3 items.
Then click the Copy button.

- ⊟ 🖳 My Computer
  - ⊞ 💾 3½ Floppy (A:)
  - ⊟ 💿 Local Disk (C:)
    - ⊞ 🗀 Documents and Settings
    - 🗀 KMaestro
    - 🗀 Paint Shop Pro
    - 🗀 Personal
    - ⊞ 🗀 Program Files

To view any subfolders, click a plus sign above.

[Make New Folder]   [Copy]   [Cancel]

You can create a new folder for the copy if you need it

Rename a file

1 Select the file and click **Rename this file** in the Tasks list.

or

2 Right-click on the file and select **Rename**.

3 Change the name and press **Enter**.

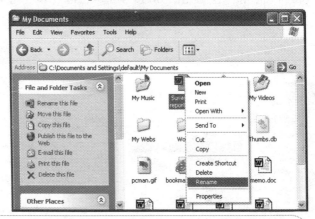

tip

When renaming files, do not change their extensions! If you do, you will lose the document–application link (page 70).

Send files elsewhere

The **Send To** command on the **File** menu (or on the shortcut menu) offers a simple way to copy a file to a floppy disk, to send one by e-mail, or to start uploading a page to your Web space.

Just select the destination to begin! Once you've started the file on its way, the rest of the process runs through as normal.

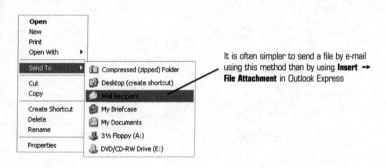

It is often simpler to send a file by e-mail using this method than by using **Insert → File Attachment** in Outlook Express

Delete files

If a file is no longer needed, select it and press the **Delete** or **Backspace** key or use the **Delete** command on the **File** menu.

Windows XP makes it very difficult to delete files by accident!

* You have to confirm – or cancel – the deletion at the prompt.
* And nothing is actually deleted at this stage. Instead, the file or folder is moved to the Recycle Bin. Let's look at that now.

tip

If you delete a folder, all its files are also deleted.

Use the Recycle Bin

The Recycle Bin allows you to recover files deleted in error. You'll rarely need it, but when you do, you will be glad that it is there!

To restore a deleted file:

1 Click the Desktop icon to open the Recycle Bin.

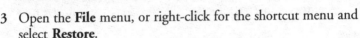

2 Select the file.

3 Open the **File** menu, or right-click for the shortcut menu and select **Restore**.

♦ If the file's folder has also been deleted, it will be re-created first, so that the file can go back where it came from.

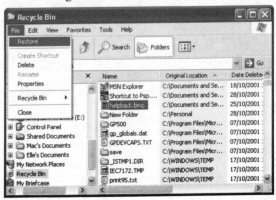

Empty the Bin

One of the main reasons for deleting files is to free up disk space, but as long as they are in the Recycle Bin, they are still on the disk. So, make a habit of emptying the Bin regularly.

1 Open the Bin and check its contents carefully and restore any accidental deletions.

2 Open the **File** menu and select **Empty Recycle Bin**.

File
Empty Recycle Bin
Create Shortcut
Delete
Rename
Properties
Recycle Bin ▶
Close

tip

The default setting lets the Recycle Bin use 10% of the drive's capacity. If you want to change this, right-click on the Bin's icon to open its Properties panel and set the level there.

Search for a file

The **Search for File or Folders** routine can track down lost files for you, hunting for them by name, location, contents, date, type and/or size.

1 In My Computer, click the Search icon .

or

2 Click **Start**, point to **Search**.

3 Select **All Files and Folders**.

4 Enter all or part of the filename or some text from within the file – or a combination of the two.

+ For example, if you were looking for a letter to 'Mr Ree', you would know that it contained his name and that it was a Word document. You could simply give 'Mr Ree' as the text, but if you type 'doc' in the filename slot, it will speed things up, as the search would then only have to check document files.

5 If you specify the drives or folders to start looking in, it will speed up the search. And note that the search will normally look into all the subfolders below the start point.

6 Click **Search** to start the search.

Enter all or part of the filename

If there are any names or special words in the
text that will identify the file, enter them here

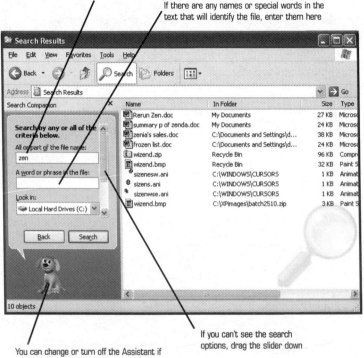

You can change or turn off the Assistant if
you prefer – right-click on it for the options

If you can't see the search
options, drag the slider down

Search for files by date

Specify the date if you know when you created or last worked on the file and you want to speed up the search.

1 Click the chevrons by **When was it modified?** to open the date options area.

2 Select an approximate date range.

or

3 Select **Specify dates**.

4 Set the dates **between** which to search.

5 Click **Search**.

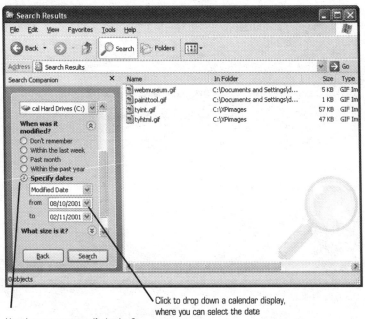

Click to drop down a calendar display, where you can select the date

How do you want to specify the date?

DATES LIMITS CAN BE SET IN SEVERAL WAYS – AND IF YOU CAN SPECIFY THE LIMITS QUITE TIGHTLY, YOU WILL GET FEWER IRRELEVANT FILES

Search for files by type or size

1 Click the chevrons by **When size is it?** to open the date options area.

2 Set an approximate size, or select **Specify size** and set the lowest and highest limits.

3 Click the chevrons by **More advanced options**.

4 In the **Type** drop-down list, select the type of file.

5 Click **Search**.

tip

You can search purely by type or size, but these options are normally used to restrict a search that otherwise might turn up too many results.

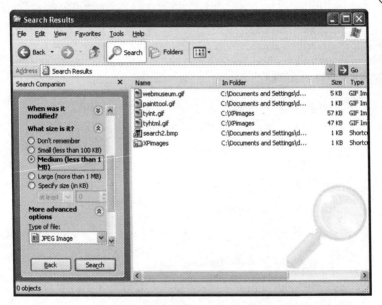

There are more options further down. These are best left at their defaults:

If you turn off **Search Subfolders**, it will only search the top level of a disk;

if you turn on **Case sensitive**, filenames must be written in the same combinations of lower-case and capital letters to match

Create shortcuts

A Desktop shortcut offers the simplest and quickest way to start an application or open a folder – as long as you can see the Desktop! You can create new shortcuts in several ways. This is probably the easiest.

Application shortcuts

1 Open the application's folder in Explorer or My Computer.

2 Locate the program file. If you are not sure whether it is the right one, click (or double-click) on it. If the application runs, it's the right file.

3 Drag the file onto the Desktop.

4 Edit the name to remove '*Shortcut to...*'.

Shortcuts to folders

1 Select the folder in Explorer or My Computer.

2 Hold the right mouse button down and drag the icon onto the Desktop.

3 Select **Create Shortcut(s) Here**.

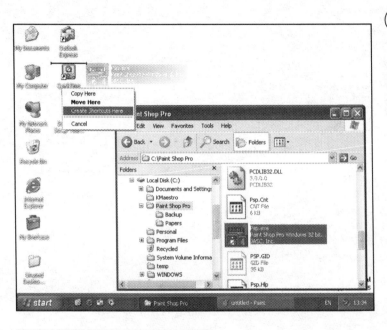

CREATING A DESKTOP SHORTCUT USING WINDOWS EXPLORER

CUSTOMIZING

The Control Panel

Open the panel

To open the Control Panel, click the **Start** button and select the **Control Panel** link in the middle of the right-hand side.

The panel has two alternative displays:

* **Category View** (opposite, top) is the default and probably the best view for new users. It groups the components by function and guides you through the tasks.

* **Classic View** (opposite, bottom) will be familiar to users of previous versions of Windows. It takes you directly to the components, and for the most part – though not always – it is obvious which you should use to customize which part of your PC.

To change between the two, click the **Switch to … View** link in the Common Tasks.

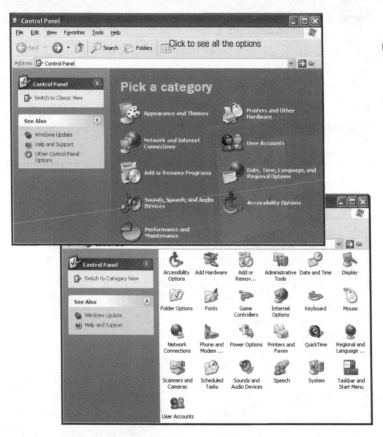

THE CONTROL PANEL

Set the date and time

Even if you do not use the Taskbar Clock, you should still make sure that the clock/calendar is correctly set if you want the date and time details to be right on your saved documents.

PCs are good time-keepers – Windows XP even adjusts for Summer Time automatically – as long as they are set correctly at the start.

Start from the **Date, Time, Language and Regional options** or click the **Date and Time** icon and check your clock.

* To change the date, select the month from the drop-down list, and click on the day.

* To change the time, select the hour digits and use the arrow buttons, then repeat with the minute and seconds digits.

* To change the time zone, go to the **Time Zone** tab and select one from the drop-down list.

Click to set

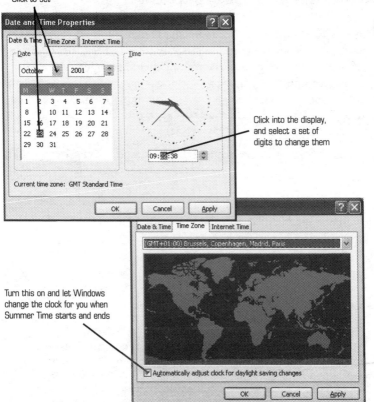

Click into the display, and select a set of digits to change them

Turn this on and let Windows change the clock for you when Summer Time starts and ends

Change the Desktop theme

A theme sets the overall style for the Desktop – its background image, the icons for the standard Windows utilities, the selection of colours and fonts, and the sounds that are triggered by events (alerts, prompts, startup and shut down, etc.). If there are parts of the theme that you don't like, you can modify them on the other tabs. The **Themes** tab in the **Display** panel simply lets you change the theme.

1 **Start from Appearance and Themes,** and select **Change the theme.**

or

2 Click the **Display** icon.

3 Select the theme from the drop-down list at the top.

4 Click **OK.**

tip

If you modify any of the settings, you can use the **Save As...** routine to save the modified theme with a new name. If someone later changes the settings, you can restore the appearance by selecting your saved theme.

Click **Apply** if you want to see the theme
in place before committing yourself

IF YOU USE ALL ASPECTS OF A THEME, THE DESKTOP WILL BE MORE CONSISTENT, BUT MAY NOT BE AS CLEAR AS
YOU MIGHT LIKE – SOME THEMES HAVE VERY DARK BACKGROUNDS, SOME HAVE HARD-TO-READ FONTS.

Adjust the Display - the Background

The background is purely decorative. It can be a plain colour, a single picture, a small image 'tiled' to fill the screen or an HTML document. Windows has some suitable images and HTML pages, but any JPG, GIF or BMP image or Web page can be used.

1 Start from **Appearance and Themes** and select **Change the background**.

or

2 Click the **Display** icon to open the **Display Properties** panel and go to the **Desktop** tab.

3 Scroll through the list of images and pages. If one sounds interesting, select it to see its preview.

♦ With a small image, set the **Display** mode to **Tile**. With a larger image, set the **Display** mode to **Center** to see it in its natural size, or **Stretch** to make it fill the screen.

4 Click **Apply** to test the choice. If you don't like it, try another.

tip

Don't click **OK** until you have worked through all the tabs. Clicking **OK** will close the Display Properties panel.

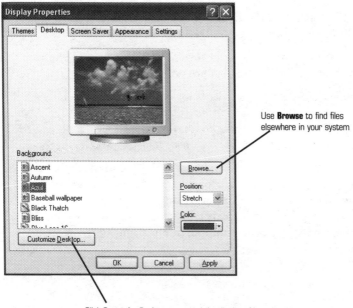

Use **Browse** to find files elsewhere in your system

Click **Customize Desktop** to control the display of icons or to set a Web page as background – see the next page

SELECTING A BACKGROUND ON THE DESKTOP TAB

Customize the Desktop

While you are on the **Desktop** tab, click the **Customize Desktop** button. This opens the **Desktop Items** panel.

On the **General** tab you can turn off the display of any of the standard Desktop icons that are not required.

You can also select new images for other icons, and – rather more usefully – you can run the Desktop Cleanup wizard. This will pick up any icons that you have not used for a long while and tuck them into an *Unused Items* folder on the Desktop.

On the Web tab, you can link to a Web page to make that the background image, and the page can be set to be updated automatically when you are online. I suspect that this will be of more interest to people who have permanently open lines to the Web and who need up-to-the-minute information from a specialist service.

If you want to use a Web page as a background, go to the **Web** tab and select the page.

Some themes have rather esoteric icons – you may want to replace them with ones that are easy to recognize

Turn this on if you want the Wizard to run automatically every 60 days

Desktop Items ?×

General | Web

Desktop icons

☑ My Documents ☐ My Network Places

☑ My Computer ☑ Internet Explorer

My Computer My Documents My Network Places Recycle Bin (full) Re (

Change Icon... Restore Default

Desktop cleanup

Desktop cleanup moves unused desktop items to a folder.

☑ Run Desktop Cleanup Wizard every 60 days

Clean Desktop Now

OK Cancel

THE **GENERAL** TAB OF THE DESKTOP ITEMS DIALOG BOX.

Change the Screen Saver

A screen saver is a moving image that takes over the screen if the computer is left unattended for a while. On older monitors this prevented a static image from burning a permanent ghost image into the screen. Newer monitors do not suffer from this – in fact, most will turn themselves off if the computer is left idle.

The screen saver can be set so that once it starts, you have enter a password (or log-on at the Welcome screen, where there are several users) before you can get back to the working screen. This password-protection can be useful if you do not want passers-by to get into your system while you are away from your desk.

1 Switch to the **Screen Saver** tab.

2 Select a saver from the drop-down list.

3 Click **Preview** for a full screen demo.

4 Click **Settings…** to set the timing, colour or other options.

5 Set the time to **Wait** before activating the saver.

6 Turn on **On resume, password protect** (or **On resume, display Welcome screen**) if wanted.

7 Click **Apply**.

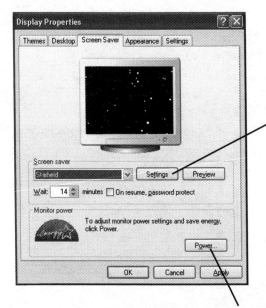

The **Settings** have options for the speed, colour, text or other features, depending on the choice of Screen Saver

If your PC has Energy saving, use this **Power ...** button to set when the screen should turn itself off. You may also be able to turn the hard disk off to save power. Both screen and hard disk will wake up and be ready, exactly as you left them, when you want to start work again

Set the Appearance

Use this panel to set the style, colour and fonts for the Desktop and standard Windows elements – the menus, dialog boxes, etc.

The main option is **Windows and buttons**.

* *Windows XP Style* offers a limited choice of colour schemes,
* *Windows Classic Style* has a very wide range of colour schemes, including several high contrast schemes for the visually impaired.

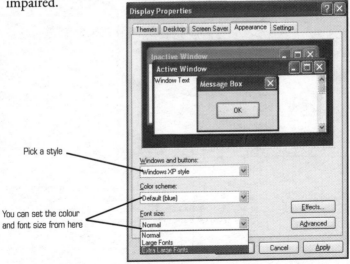

Pick a style

You can set the colour and font size from here

With any scheme you can adjust the size, colour and font of individual elements through the **Advanced Appearance** dialog box.

1 Click the **Advanced** button to open the dialog box.

2 Click on an item in the preview pane, or select it from the Item drop-down list.

3 Set its size and colour, and font attributes as required.

4 Click **OK** to return to the **Properties** panel.

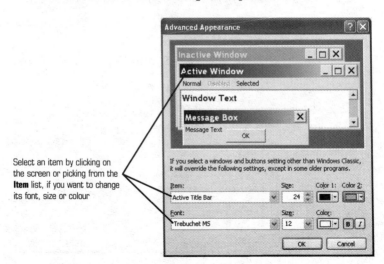

Select an item by clicking on the screen or picking from the **Item** list, if you want to change its font, size or colour

Adjust the Effects

The **Effects** dialog box, reached from the **Effects** button on the Appearance tab, contains only one significant option – turn on **Use large icons** if you need the extra visibility. The other options are largely decorative.

1 Click the **Effects** button on the **Appearance** tab.

2 Set the effects to your own liking – most have little practical effect, except possibly slowing down your PC.

3 Click **Apply**.

These improve the display, but may slow things down a fraction

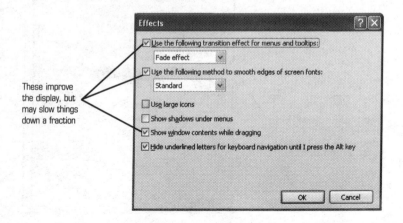

Adjust the Settings

The Settings relate to the size of the screen and number of colours used in the display. They should normally be left alone as Windows XP will select the optimum settings for your system – and the **Advanced** settings should certainly be left at their defaults unless you know and understand the details of your system. Bad selections here can really mess up your screen!

The Screen resolution is set low as this works better for the small pictures I need for this book. 1280 × 1024 or higher makes better use of a 19" monitor

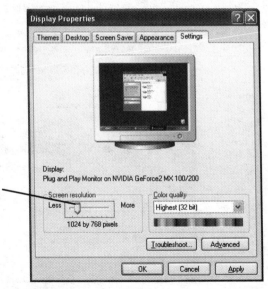

Add or remove a program

New programs should be installed through their setup routines. Use this panel to *uninstall* software. If you just delete a program's folder, it may remove all or most of its files – but not the Start menu entry or the File Types associations.

1 Click **Add or Remove Programs**.

2 Select the program and Click **Change/Remove…**

3 With some software you can then select which components to uninstall; with others the whole package is simply removed.

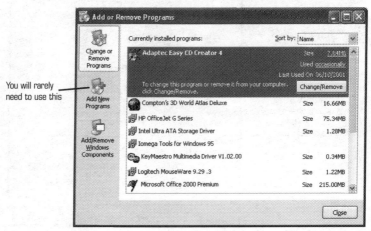

You will rarely need to use this

Adjust the Windows Setup

Some of the components of Windows XP are optional, and can be removed (or replaced) at any time.

1 Go to the **Windows Setup** tab of **Add or Remove Programs**.

2 Select a **Component** and click **Details…**

3 Tick the checkbox to add a component, or clear it to remove an existing one, then click **OK**.

4 Click **OK** when you have done, and wait while Windows adds or removes components. You may have to restart the PC.

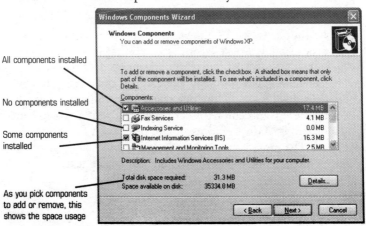

All components installed

No components installed

Some components installed

As you pick components to add or remove, this shows the space usage

Understand fonts

A font is a typeface design, identified by a name. Within one font
you will get type in a range of sizes, and the appearance may be
varied by the use of bold, italic or other styles.

Fonts can be divided into three categories:

* **Serif** – like this (Garamond), have little tails (serifs) at the
  ends of strokes.

* **Sans serif** – like this (Arial), with simpler lines.

* Display – *decorative* **fonts** of all kinds.

There are thousands of fonts, and a couple of dozen of the best of
these are supplied with Windows XP. You will get more with any
word-processing and page layout software that you install, and
you can buy CDs full of fonts. You do not need a huge number.
Professional designers normally work to the 'three-font' rule: no
more than three fonts on any one page, using different sizes and
styles for variety and emphasis. Three or four serif and sans fonts
and a dozen or so display fonts should be enough for most
purposes. The more you have, the longer it will take to scroll
through the font list whenever you are formatting text!

Display your fonts

1 Start from **Appearance and Themes** and click the **Fonts** folder link on the left.

2 Click 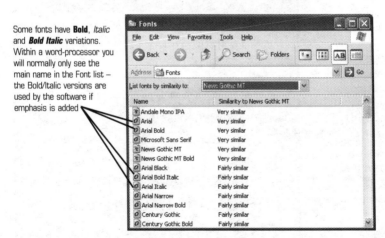 to list the fonts by similarity, then choose a font from the drop-down list. If you have a lot of very similar fonts, you might think about getting rid of some.

3 Or click for large icons, or for a list display.

Some fonts have **Bold**, *Italic* and ***Bold Italic*** variations. Within a word-processor you will normally only see the main name in the Font list – the Bold/Italic versions are used by the software if emphasis is added

IN THE **LIST BY SIMILARITY** VIEW, FONTS ARE LISTED IN ORDER OF CLOSENESS OF MATCH TO THE SELECTED FONT

View a font

1 Open the **Fonts** folder.

2 Click the font. A viewer will open, showing samples of text in a range of sizes.

3 If you want a printed copy for closer checking, click **Print**.

4 Click **Done** or ☒ to close the viewer.

You can view several fonts at once if you want to compare them side by side. The viewer opens in the same place on screen – move it to see the font below.

News Gothic MT (TrueType)

Done   Print

News Gothic MT (TrueType)

Typeface name: News Gothic MT
File size: 65 KB
Version: Version 1.00
Design and data by The Monotype Corporation. © 1993. Microsoft Corporation. All rights reserved.

abcdefghijklmnopqrstuvwxyz
ABCDEFGHIJKLMNOPQRSTUVWXYZ
123456789.:,;(:*!?')

12 The quick brown fox jumps over the lazy dog. 1234567890

18 The quick brown fox jumps over the lazy dog. 1

24 The quick brown fox jumps over the

36 The quick brown fox jum

48 The quick brown f

Install fonts

If you have fonts on CD-ROM or have downloaded them from the Internet, they must be installed before they can be used.

1 Open the **File** menu and select **Install New Font**.

2 At the **Add Fonts** panel, select the drive and folder.

3 Select the fonts from the list, holding down **Control** while you click if you want to pick several.

4 If the font file is already on your hard disk, clear the **Copy fonts to Fonts folder** checkbox.

5 Click **OK**.

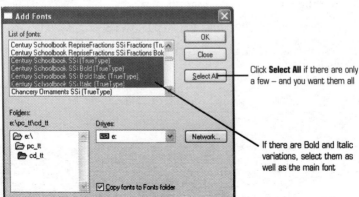

Click **Select All** if there are only a few – and you want them all

If there are Bold and Italic variations, select them as well as the main font

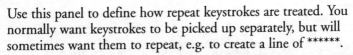
Adjust the keyboard

Use this panel to define how repeat keystrokes are treated. You normally want keystrokes to be picked up separately, but will sometimes want them to repeat, e.g. to create a line of ******.

- The **Repeat delay** is how long to wait before starting to repeat – if you are heavy-fingered, set this to *Long*.

- The **Repeat rate** is how fast the characters are produced. This should match your reaction times.

1 Start from **Printers and Other Hardware** and click the **Keyboard** icon.

2 Test the settings by typing in the test area.

3 Move the sliders to adjust the **Repeat delay** and **Repeat rate**.

4 Test and adjust until the keys respond as you would like, then click **OK**.

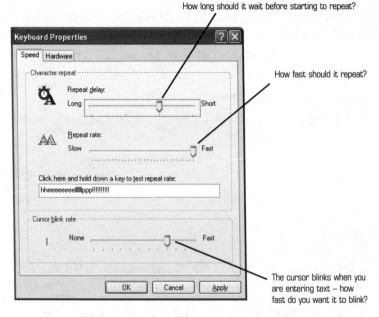

How long should it wait before starting to repeat?

How fast should it repeat?

The cursor blinks when you are entering text – how fast do you want it to blink?

Configure the mouse buttons

The only crucial setting here is the **Double-click** speed – you need to be able to double-click reliably!

1   Start from **Printers and Other Hardware** and click the **Mouse** icon.

2   Make sure that the **Buttons** tab is at the front.

3   Test the setting by double-clicking on the folder image to make it open and close.

4   Move the slider to adjust the response if necessary.

5   Click **Apply** – not **OK** as we want to use the other tabs.

tip

You can switch the buttons over if you are left-handed, but it is better to get used to the standard layout, unless this is the only PC you use and only you ever use it. (Switching to the left-handed layout will also thoroughly confuse anyone else who tries to use the machine!)

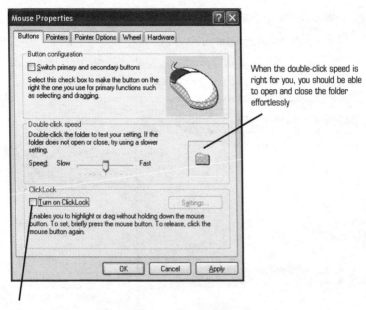

When the double-click speed is right for you, you should be able to open and close the folder effortlessly

If you find dragging difficult, try turning on ClickLock. With this on, when you need to drag something, hold down the button for a moment and it will behave as if it is being held down – click as normal to release the lock

Pick your pointers

1 Switch to the **Pointers** tab.

2 Pick a **Scheme** from the drop-down list.

3 To change a single pointer, select it and click **Browse**. You can then pick a new one from the pointers folder.

4 Click **Apply**.

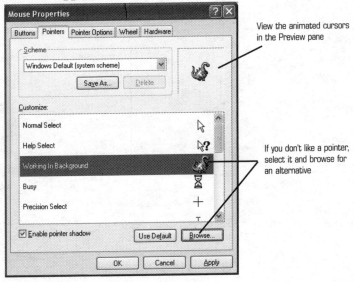

View the animated cursors in the Preview pane

If you don't like a pointer, select it and browse for an alternative

Set other pointer options

The **Pointer speed** controls how the pointer moves in relation to the mouse.

1 If you don't feel in control of the mouse, drag the slider towards **Slow**.

2 If it's taking too long to get around the screen, set it faster.

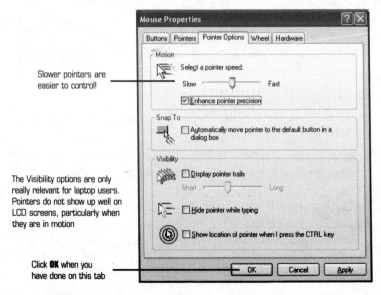

Slower pointers are easier to control!

The Visibility options are only really relevant for laptop users. Pointers do not show up well on LCD screens, particularly when they are in motion

Click **OK** when you have done on this tab

Add another language keyboard

Windows XP allows you to set up the
keyboard for entering text in another
language, and to switch between this and
your standard keyboard through the
Language Bar.

The link opens at the **Languages** tab of
the **Regional and Language Options** panel. Here's how to to add
a new language.

1 Start from the **Date, Time, Language and Regional options**
   and select **Add other languages**.

2 Click the **Details...** button.

3 At the **Text Services and Input Languages** dialog box, click
   Add then select the language.

• If you want to be able to switch using keyboard shortcuts,
   click on **Key Settings** and define the shortcuts.

This facility is best suited to touch-typists who are used to a
foreign keyboard – most of us will be better off selecting
accented letters,etc. from the Character Map (page 216).

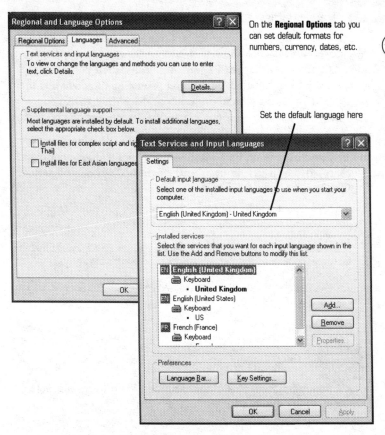

On the **Regional Options** tab you can set default formats for numbers, currency, dates, etc.

THE CONTROL PANEL

Set the default language here

Regional and Language Options ?✕

Regional Options | Languages | Advanced

Text services and input languages
To view or change the languages and methods you can use to enter text, click Details.

Details...

Supplemental language support
Most languages are installed by default. To install additional languages, select the appropriate check box below.

☐ Install files for complex script and right-to-left languages (including Thai)

☐ Install files for East Asian languages

OK

Text Services and Input Languages ?✕

Settings

Default input language
Select one of the installed input languages to use when you start your computer.

English (United Kingdom) - United Kingdom ▾

Installed services
Select the services that you want for each input language shown in the list. Use the Add and Remove buttons to modify this list.

EN English (United Kingdom)
  ⌨ Keyboard
    • **United Kingdom**
EN English (United States)
  ⌨ Keyboard
    • US
FR French (France)
  ⌨ Keyboard

Add...
Remove
Properties

Preferences

Language Bar... | Key Settings...

OK | Cancel | Apply

Change the sounds

Windows can attach sounds to events so that you get, for example a fanfare at start up and a warning noise when you are about to do something you may later regret. Some of these are just for fun; but if you tend to watch the keyboard, rather than the screen, when you are typing, then audible warnings can be useful.

The Sounds Properties panel is where you decide which events are to be accompanied by a sound, and which sounds to use.

1 Start from **Sounds, Speech and Audion devices**, and select **Change the sound scheme**.

2 Select a **Sound Scheme** from the list. You can then check – and change – sounds for individual events.

3 If an event has ● to its left, it has a sound attached. Click ▶ to hear it.

4 To change the sound, select the event and click **Browse** and pick a new sound file.

5 Click **Apply**.

The other tabs control the devices used for multimedia work. It's best to let the system sort these out.

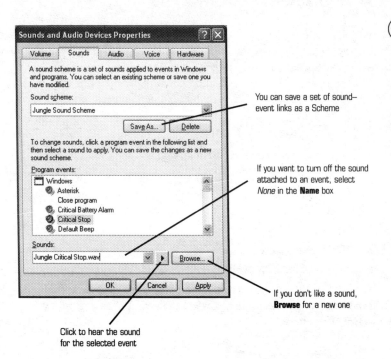

You can save a set of sound–event links as a Scheme

If you want to turn off the sound attached to an event, select *None* in the **Name** box

If you don't like a sound, **Browse** for a new one

Click to hear the sound for the selected event

Add a user

Windows XP makes it easy for several people to share the use of one PC. Each user can have their own set of folders and their own customized Desktop and Start menu. Here's how to set up an account for a new user.

1 Click the **User Accounts** link in the Control Panel.

2 Click **Create a new account**.

3 Enter the user's name and click **Next**.

4 Set the account type. As some older Windows software may not run properly with the 'Limited' type, users should be set as 'Administrators' unless it is important to restrict their access.

5 Click **Create Account**.

That's all there is to it at this stage. The new user can later set, change or remove a password, change the picture or set up a .NET password – a single password that can be used at many secure Web sites.

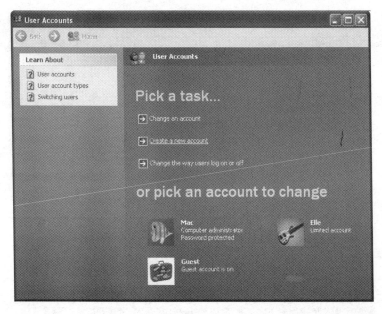

THE **USER ACCOUNTS** PANEL AS SEEN BY AN ADMINISTRATOR. FROM HERE AN ADMINISTRATOR CAN CREATE NEW ACCOUNTS, CHANGE THE SETTINGS FOR AN EXISTING ACCOUNT OR DELETE UNWANTED ONES.

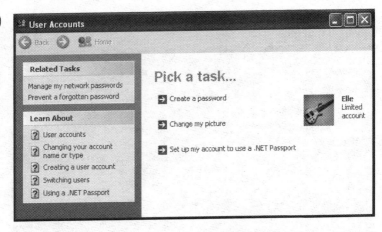

THE **USER ACCOUNTS** PANEL BELONGING TO A LIMITED USER. THESE USERS CAN CHANGE THEIR PASSWORDS AND PICTURES, AND SET UP A .NET PASSPORT, BUT HAVE NO OTHER CONTROL.

THE PICTURE CAN BE CHANGED EASILY AND WHENEVER REQUIRED.

PASSWORDS SHOULD ONLY BE CREATED IF NEEDED – THEY CAN BE A PAIN. IF YOU DO CREATE ONE, CLICK THE **PREVENT A FORGOTTEN PASSWORD** LINK IN THE RELATED TASKS AND CREATE A 'PASSWORD RESET' DISK. THIS WILL ENABLE YOU TO RECOVER ALL YOUR DATA SHOULD YOU LATER FORGET THE PASSWORD.

Improve Accessibility

The options can be set through the **Configure Windows...**
wizard or more directly through the **Accessibility Options** panel.
Click the **Accessibility Options** icon to open the panel.

If you turn an option on, click its **Settings** button to open a
dialog box where you can adjust it to your needs.

Keyboard

StickyKeys will 'hold down'
the **Shift**, **Ctrl** or **Alt** keys
while you press the next to
get a keyboard shortcut
combination.

FilterKeys control the point
at which keystrokes are
picked up, or are repeated,
and the repeat rate (see page
124).

ToggleKeys will make
sounds when the **Caps
Lock**, **Num Lock** or **Scroll
Lock** keys are pressed.

Sound

The main option on this tab turns on visual clues to replace or emphasize sound prompts.

Display

The high contrast display options, which are also available in the *Windows Classic* colour schemes on the **Display Properties** panel (page 114), can be turned on here.

Mouse

The **MouseKeys** option lets the Number pad keys mimic mouse actions. The central key (5) is the left click; minus and 5 are the right-click; the numbers (7, 8, 9, 4, 6, 1, 2, 3) move the mouse.

General

If you have set up an accessibility option so that it can be toggled on and off as required, go to this tab to define when to turn options off, and how to notify you of their status. If you have a device plugged into your serial port, to use in place of the standard keyboard or mouse, it can be set up through this tab.

The Taskbar and Start menu

Set Taskbar options

Right-click anywhere on a blank area of the Taskbar and select **Properties** to open the panel.

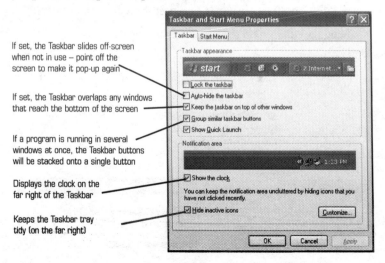

If set, the Taskbar slides off-screen when not in use – point off the screen to make it pop-up again

If set, the Taskbar overlaps any windows that reach the bottom of the screen

If a program is running in several windows at once, the Taskbar buttons will be stacked onto a single button

Displays the clock on the far right of the Taskbar

Keeps the Taskbar tray tidy (on the far right)

Display toolbars

In its initial settings, the Taskbar has two toolbars on it – **Quick Launch** (see page 21) and **Language Bar** (page 130). More can be added if you want to be able to start more applications from the Taskbar. There are five ready-made toolbars.

- **Address** – enter an Internet address here, and Internet Explorer will start and try to connect to it.

- **Links** – carries a set of buttons with Internet addresses: clicking one starts Internet Explorer, to make the connection.

- **Language Bar** – sets the keyboard's language.

- **Desktop** – contains copies of the icons present on the Desktop.

- **Quick Launch** – for starting the main Internet applications.

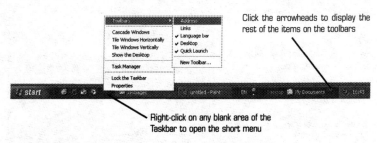

Click the arrowheads to display the rest of the items on the toolbars

Right-click on any blank area of the Taskbar to open the short menu

THE TASKBAR WITH THE QUICK LAUNCH, DESKTOP AND LANGAUGE BAR TOOLBARS

Change a toolbar's options

The short menu that can be opened from a toolbar contains the usual Taskbar items, plus some options for the toolbar. Most of these are at the top of the menu.

View → Large or **Small** sets the icon size.

Open folder opens the toolbar's folder so that you can add or remove shortcuts.

Refresh simply redraws the toolbar.

Show Title displays the toolbar's title.

Close closes the toolbar – you will be prompted to confirm this.

Create a toolbar

You can set up your own toolbars with shortcuts to applications, folders or Internet links:

1 Create a folder, within My Documents, and name it 'My Tools' or something similar.

2 Set up shortcuts (see page 98) to your applications or folders.

3 If you are going to show text labels on the toolbar, edit the names so that they are as brief as possible.

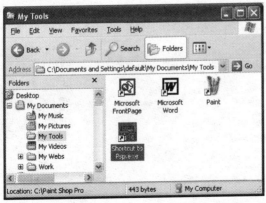

THE NEW TOOLBAR FOLDER, ALMOST READY TO BE ADDED TO THE TASKBAR – THE PAINT SHOP PRO (PSP.EXE) SHORTCUT NAME NEEDS EDITING

4 When you have assembled your shortcuts, right-click on the **Taskbar**, point to **Toolbars** and select **New Toolbar...**

5 Work through the folder display to find the one containing your shortcuts.

6 Click **OK**.

New Toolbar

Choose a folder, or type an Internet address

- Desktop
  - My Documents
    - My Music
    - My Pictures
    - My Tools
    - My Videos
    - My Webs
    - Work

Browse to the new toolbar folder

Folder: My Tools

[Make New Folder]   [OK]   [Cancel]

Resize the Taskbar

The Taskbar is normally a thin bar across the bottom of the screen, which is fine when it is used only for the Quick Launch toolbar and a few application buttons. Add more toolbars and it is going to get crowded and difficult to use.

One possible solution is to make the Taskbar deeper by dragging its top edge upwards.

The toolbars can be rearranged within this area by dragging on their handles. Move them up or down between the lines, or drag sideways to adjust their relative sizes.

◆ Before you start, right-click on the Taskbar and make sure that the **Lock the Taskbar** option is turned off.

Drag the edge to change the depth

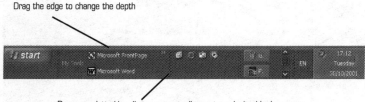

Drag on a dotted handle to move a toolbar or to make it wider/narrower

Move the Taskbar

A second solution is to move the Taskbar to one or other side of the screen. By default it will be wide enough to show the Text labels on the icons.

1 Click onto the Taskbar in the space to the right of the application buttons.

2 Drag the Taskbar up to the side.

3 Drag on the handles between the sections to adjust the layout.

4 Drag the edge inwards if you want to make the bar slimmer.

Click into this space to drag the Taskbar

Customize the Start menu

The most dramatic change you can make to the menu is to switch to the 'Classic' style. This option is mainly for experienced users of earlier versions of Windows. We will stick with the new XP Start menu. There are some simple, and some slightly more complicated, things you can do to customize this.

1 Right-click on the **Start** button and select **Properties** from the short menu, to go to the **Start Menu** tab.

2 Click **Customize...**

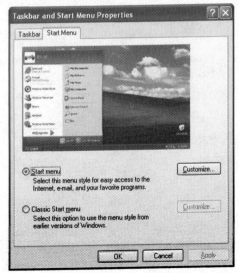

3 At the **Customize Start Menu** dialog box, select the icon size.

4 In the **Programs** area, set how many shortcuts to have in the quick access set on the left – you may want more or less.

5 You can select the programs to run from the **Internet** and the **E-mail** shortcuts, or turn them off if not wanted.

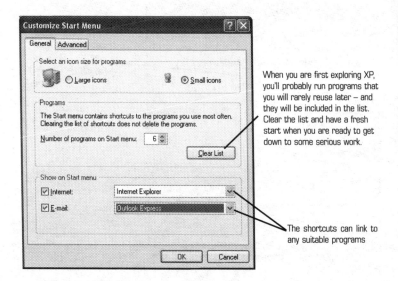

When you are first exploring XP, you'll probably run programs that you will rarely reuse later – and they will be included in the list. Clear the list and have a fresh start when you are ready to get down to some serious work.

The shortcuts can link to any suitable programs

FIRST STEPS IN CUSTOMIZING THE START MENU.

6 On the **Advanced** tab you control which of the standard shortcuts are displayed on the right side of the menu. All can be turned off if not required. Work through the **Start menu items** list, setting items to be displayed or not.

7 Click **OK**.

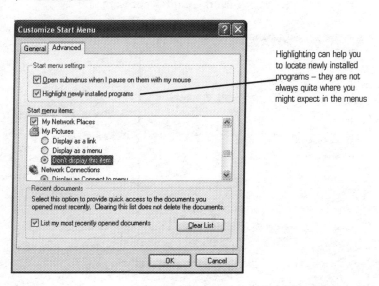

Highlighting can help you to locate newly installed programs – they are not always quite where you might expect in the menus

THE **ADVANCED** TAB ALLOWS YOU TO CONTROL WHICH OF THE STANDARD SHORTCUTS ARE DISPLAYED.

Reorganize the menus

The Start menu system is stored as a set of folders and subfolders – or rather, as several sets, as each user has his or her own Start menu. Within the Start menu are folders for each submenu, and the shortcuts are held as files in these.

If you have installed so many applications that your **All Programs** menu has become overcrowded, create group folders and move the shortcuts and folders of related applications into these. A short main menu that leads to two levels of submenus is easier to work with than one huge menu!

1 Open the Start menu, right-click on **All Programs** and select **Open** from the short menu.

2 When the Start menu folder opens, click **Folders** to display the folder list – it will make it much easier to see what you are doing.

3 Reorganize the menu system, using the normal file management techniques for moving, deleting and renaming files (shortcuts) and folders (submenus).

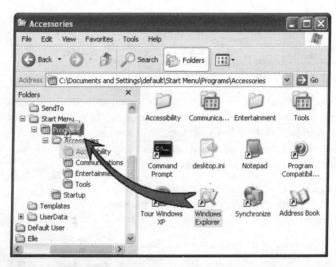

EXPLORING THE FOLDERS OF THE START MENU SYSTEM. IN THE EXAMPLE, *WINDOWS EXPLORER* IS BEING MOVED TO THE MAIN PROGRAMS MENU – THIS IS A USEFUL PROGRAM AND SHOULD BE EASY TO GET TO.

MANAGING YOUR PC

Printers

Add a printer

If your printer dates from before Autumn 2001, the drivers – the programs that convert computer files into the right form for printing – on the Windows XP CD are probably newer than those supplied with the printer. If it is more recent, dig out its installation disk.

The **Add Printer Wizard** makes installation simple.

1 Open the **Printers** folder, from the **Start** menu.

2 Click **Add Printer** to run the wizard.

This system has several printers – the OfficeJet is the default (shown by ✓); BigMac's Brother is on the network

3 At the first screen, select *Local printer*, if it is attached to your PC, or *Network printer* if you are on a Network and the printer is attached to another PC. Turn off the *Automatically detect and install option* – if it was going to work, it would have done so already!

4 For a local printer, choose the port – normally LPT1.

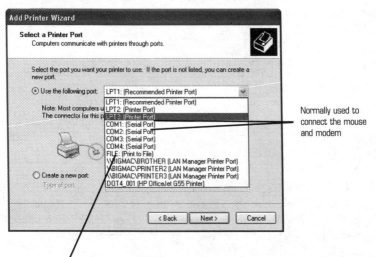

Normally used to connect the mouse and modem

FILE is used if you are outputting files for remote printing, e.g. at a commercial printer's

5 For a network printer, browse the network to find the printer you want to use.

Click the computer icon to see its printers

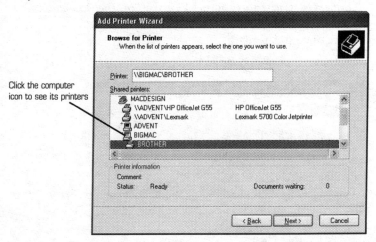

6 If you are using a Windows driver, select the **Manufacturer** from the list, then the **Printer** model. If you are using the drivers supplied with the printer, click **Have Disk**, then select the model from the list that is drawn from the disk.

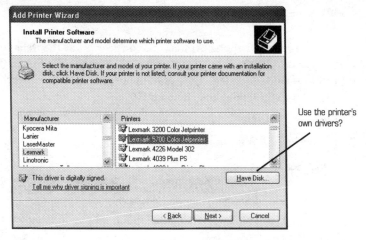

Use the printer's own drivers?

7 You may want to edit the full manufacturer/model name into something shorter to label the icon in the Printers folder.

8 At the final stage, accept the offer of a test print – it's as well to check! Once you click **Finish**, the Wizard will load the driver from the disk and install it in your system.

Set the default printer

If you have more than one printer, one must be set as the default. This is the one that will be used if you click a program's Print button to print something. To choose the printer, you must work through the Print dialog box (see page 161).

1 Open the **Printers** folder.

2 Right-click on the printer.

3 Select **Set as Default**.

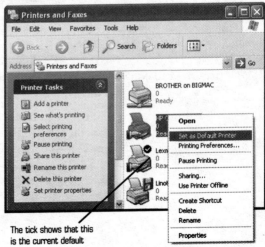

The tick shows that this is the current default

Printer properties

Right-click on the icon in the Printers folder and select **Properties**. Different printers have different panels, but you should find:

- A **General** tab, where you can type a comment – this may be useful on a network.

- A **Sharing** tab, if you are on a network.

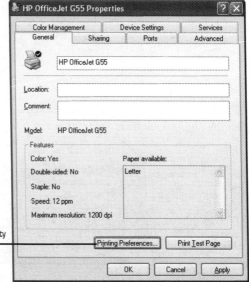

Set the defaults layout and quality preferences (see page 159)

- An **Advanced** tab, where you can select a new driver if needed. The **Spool** settings determine whether the file is sent directly to the printer, or through a memory buffer. Spooling frees up applications, as they can send data out faster than the printer can handle it.

- A **Device Settings** tab. Check the **Memory** (normally only on laser printers). If you have added extra memory, tell Windows.

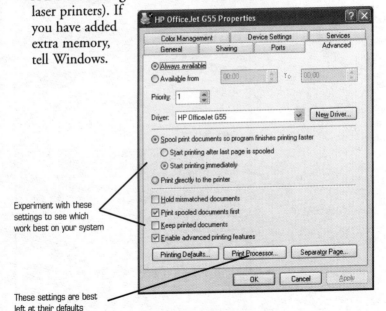

Experiment with these settings to see which work best on your system

These settings are best left at their defaults

- Colour printers have a **Color Management** tab where you can adjust the color profile – this is best left on Automatic!

- On one tab there will be a **Printing Defaults** or **Preferences** button, which leads to a dialog box where you can set the paper size, type and orientation, and the default quality level.

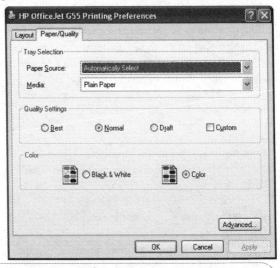

The defaults can be changed in the application before printing.

Print from within an application

The Print routines in applications are all much the same. There will usually be a toolbar button, and clicking on this will send the document to the printer using its current settings – whatever they are.

The first time that you print something, it is best to start by selecting **Print** from the **File** menu. This will open a dialog box where you can define the settings. The key settings are which pages to print and how many copies.

tip

If you need to change the layout, print quality or other printer settings, click the **Properties** button to open the printer Properties panel – this may look slightly different from the panel opened from the Printers folder, but gives you access to the same settings.

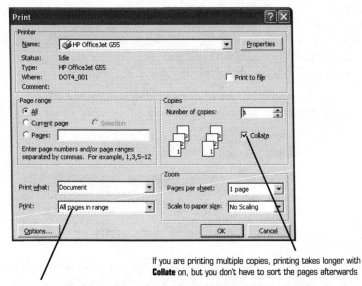

If you are printing multiple copies, printing takes longer with
Collate on, but you don't have to sort the pages afterwards

For double-sided printing, print the Odd pages first, then put the paper back in,
turn on Reverse printing (it's on Word's options) and print the Even pages

THE PRINT DIALOG BOX FROM WORD. OTHER APPLICATIONS HAVE DIFFERENT OPTIONS, BUT **PAGE RANGE** AND
COPIES ARE COMMON TO ALL

Control the print queue

When a document is sent for printing, it goes first to the print queue. If it is the only print job, it is processed directly. If not, it will sit in the queue and wait its turn. As long as a document is in the queue, you can do something about it.

* If you discover a late error, so that printing would be just a waste of paper, a job can be cancelled.

* If you have sent a series of documents in succession, you can change the order in which they are printed.

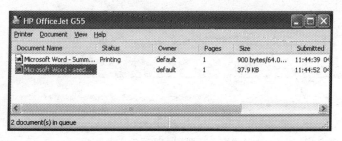

YOU CAN CANCEL A DOCUMENT AFTER IT HAS STARTED PRINTING.

When the printer is active, you will see on the right of the Taskbar, next to the clock. Click on it to open the printer's folder, where the queue is stored.

- *To cancel a print job*, select the document, then use **Cancel** from the **Document** menu.

- *To cancel all the queued jobs*, use **Cancel All Documents** from the **Printer** menu.

- *To change the order of printing*, select a document and drag it up or down the queue as required – this only works with those documents that are not already being spooled or printed.

tip

As printers can store some pages in their own memories, printing may continue for a while after you have cancelled a job. The only solution is to turn off the printer – but don't do this while a sheet is part-way through or you'll cause a jam.

Print a document from its file

If you have Windows Explorer or My Computer open, you can print a document directly from there, as long as you have an associated application which can handle it. Windows XP will open the application, print the document, then close the application for you.

To send the document to the default printer:

• Select the file and click **Print this file** in the **Common Tasks**.

or

• Right-click on the file and select **Print** from the short menu.

> ### tip
> You can print directly to any printer if you open the **Printer and Faxes** folder and the document's folder, then drag the document across the screen and drop it onto the printer icon.

YOU CAN SEND A DOCUMENT TO THE DEFAULT PRINTER DIRECTLY FROM ITS FILE, BY SELECTING PRINT FROM THE SHORT MENU OR THE COMMON TASKS.

Housekeeping

Find the System Tools

These can be reached from the **Start** button, through **Programs** → **Accessories** → **System Tools**. Open the **System Tools** menu and see what's there. You may well have a slightly different set from the one shown here.

Disk Cleanup, Disk Defragmenter, Error-checking and Backup can also be run from a disk's Properties panel. Get to know these, as well-maintained disks are essential for a reliable system.

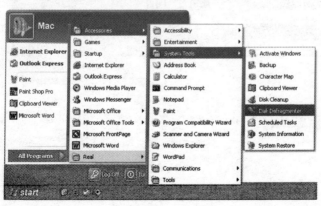

Disks and drives

These words are often used interchangeably but, strictly speaking, a disk is that flat, round thing on which data is stored, while a drive is a logical area of storage identified by a letter (A:, C:, etc). The A: drive can have different disks put into it. A hard disk can be 'partitioned' to create two or more drives.

A disk – hard or floppy – is divided into *clusters*, each of which can contain all of a small file or part of a larger one. When a file is first written to a new disk, it will be stored in a continuous sequence of clusters, and the disk will gradually fill up from the start. If a file is edited and resaved – bigger than before – it will overwrite the original clusters then write the remainder in the next available clusters, which may well not be physically next to them on the disk. When a file is deleted, it will create a space in the middle of the used area, which later may be filled by a part of another file. Over time disks get messier, with files increasingly stored in scattered clusters. A file that is held in one continuous chunk can be opened much more quickly, simply because the system does not have to chase around all over the disk to read it.

View a disk's properties

If you right-click on any drive in My Computer, and select
Properties from the menu, its Properties panel will open.

+ The **General** tab shows how much used and free space you
have on the drive.

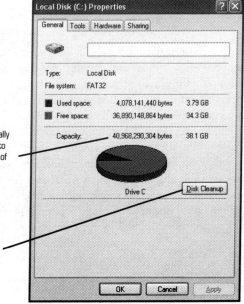

Hard drives on new PCs are typically
20Gb or larger – you'll only start to
run out of space if you store a lot of
images, or audio or video clips

Remove unwanted files – this
makes it simpler to find the
ones you do want, as well as
freeing up more space

- The **Tools** tab has buttons to start Erorr-checking, Disk Defragmenter and Backup.

- The **Hardware** tab carries technical information.

- The **Sharing** tab is only present on a network (page 194).

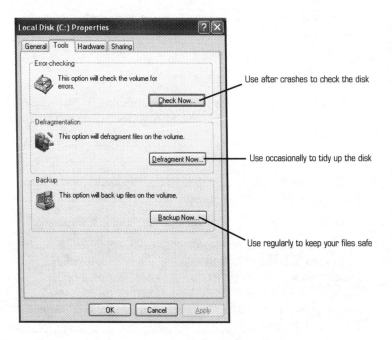

Use after crashes to check the disk

Use occasionally to tidy up the disk

Use regularly to keep your files safe

Clean up a hard disk

Disk Cleanup removes temporary and other unwanted files from the hard disk. Run it regularly to free up space and keep the clutter down.

1 Start **Disk Cleanup**, either from the **System Tools** menu or the **General** tab of the **Properties** panel.

2 Select the drive – normally **C:**.

3 Select the sets of files to delete. The key ones are:

♦ **Temporary Internet Files** – don't remove these if you will be revisiting pages, or you will have to download them again.

♦ **Downloaded Program Files** refer to applets from Web pages that were stored on your disk so that they could be run.

♦ **Offline Web Pages** – pages that were downloaded and stored for reading offline. (See *Quick Fix Internet Explorer 5.5*.)

♦ **Recycle Bin** – saves you having to empty the Bin separately.

♦ **Temporary Files** refers to those created by applications, such as automatic backups and print files. They are normally cleaned up when the application is closed, but may be left behind if it ends with a crash. Disk Cleanup will not touch any of today's files, which the application may still be using.

- **Temporary PC Health Files** are surplus copies of files used by the System Restore routines (page 180) and can be cleared.

4 Click **OK**. You will be prompted to confirm the deletions – they are irreversible – before the cleanup starts.

On the **More Options** tab you can remove unwanted Windows components or programs

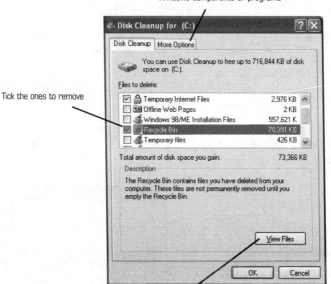

Tick the ones to remove

If you are not sure, check the files before marking the set for deletion

Check a disk for errors

In earlier Windows, the error-checker was quite complex to use, but offered good control of what to do about any errors that it found. The new error-checker is very simple, with only two options at the start, and nothing for you to do once it's running. In fact, once it's running you can't do *anything* on the PC.

◆ If no option is set, the routine simply checks that the files are stored safely. You can set one or other of these options.

◆ With **Automatically fix file system errors** on, the routine will try to solve any problems that it meets – and as it will almost certainly do this better than you or me, I'd leave it to it!

◆ The **Scan for and attempt recovery of bad sectors** will fix file system errors and also test the surface of the disk, to make sure that files can be stored safely, and rebuild it if necessary.

Error-checking in progress. Phase 1 is quite fast; Phase 2 takes ages on a big disk – go and have a coffee while it works.

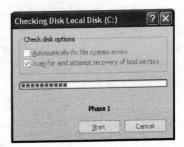

Defragment your disks

Disk Defragmenter reorganizes the physical storage of files on the
disk, pulling together the data from scattered clusters. Though it
improves performance, the gains are in the order of a few seconds
for starting a program or loading a data file, and it is a very slow
job – allow an hour or more on a 20Gb disk. It is only worth
doing regularly if your disk is getting full – so that new files are
being stored in a limited area – or if you have a high turnover of
files from working on large databases or reports, or from installing and removing demos, shareware and other programs.

1 If a program writes to the disk while Disk Defragmenter is
   running, it will restart from scratch. Close any applications
   that may create temporary files – this includes the screensaver,
   so turn that off through the Desktop's Properties panel.

2 Start Disk Defragmenter from the **System Tools** menu or
   from the **Tools** tab of the disk's **Properties** panel.

3 Select the drive, if you have a choice.

4 Click **Analyze** and wait for the report.

5 If the report recommends defragmenting, then click
   Defragment.

6 When you get bored, go and do something else for an hour.

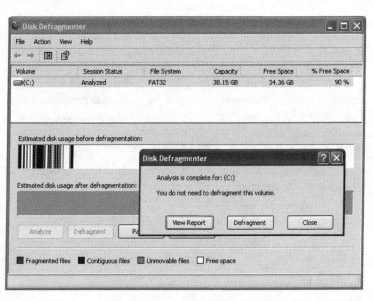

ALWAYS ANALYZE FIRST. YOU DO NOT WANT TO RUN A DEFRAGMENT UNLESS YOU HAVE TO – IT TAKES TOO LONG!

Backup your files

If an application's program files become corrupted or deleted, it is a nuisance but not a major problem as you can simply reinstall the application from the original disks. Data files are a different matter. How much is your data worth to you? How long would it take you to rewrite that report, redraw that picture or re-enter the last six months' accounts if they were lost? Individual files can be copied onto floppies for safekeeping, but if you have more than one or two it is simpler to use the Backup program. A backup job is easily set up, doesn't take long to run and will more than pay for itself in time and trouble the first time that you need it!

Backup media

Backups can be done on floppy disks, and this is fine for home use or in a small business where there's not a lot to backup – with compression, over 2Mb of data will fit on one disk. If you intend to backup large quantities of data regularly, invest £100 or so in a tape drive or an IOmega removable hard disk system – it will be far easier than struggling with a pile of floppies.

Whatever you save on must be removable. You must be able to store the backup away from the machine – in a fireproof safe or a different building if you want real security.

The Backup or Restore Wizard

When you start the wizard, you will be asked if you want to back up files or restore them from a backup. Select **Back up**.

1 If you want a backup of everything on the PC, select **All information...** Don't do this if you are backing up on floppies!

2 If you opt to back up selected files and folders, you will be given an Explorer-style display. Click the ⊞ icons to open out the folders as necessary.

Simply tick a folder if you want to back up everything in it.

If you select a folder, all its contents are selected – click on the folder name to list its contents if you only want to back up selected files, then tick those that you want

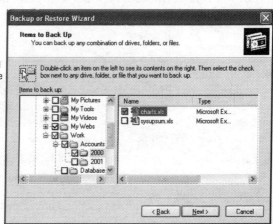

To select items within a folder, click on its name to open it, then tick individual items.

3 Select the medium (tape, disk, etc.) and drive if saving to disk, and give your backup job a name – this should describe the file selection and the date.

4 At the next – and normally final – stage, you will see a summary of the backup settings. If everything is OK, click **Finish**. If you are backing up a lot of data on to floppies, you should now sit ready to change the disks on request.

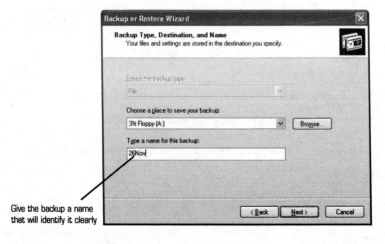

Give the backup a name that will identify it clearly

Advanced Backup settings

The **Advanced** button on the summary panel will let you set more options.

The **Type of Backup** can be:

* **Normal**, which copies all the selected files and marks them as backed up;

* **Copy**, which copies all the selected files, but without marking them as backed up;

* **Incremental** saves only those changed since last the Normal backup;

* **Differential** also saves only changed files, but without marking them as backed up;

* **Daily** saves only files created on the current day.

At the following stages you can specify the nature, placing and scheduling of the backup. If you are using a backup tape or other high capacity media, it makes sense to run the backup after you have finished work for the day.

Restore files from a backup

With any luck this will never be necessary!

1 Run **Backup**, and select **Restore** at the opening panel.

2 Insert the disk or tape with the backup into its drive.

3 Select the backup file.

4 Open the folders as necessary until you can see the files and folders that you want to restore. Tick to select them.

5 Click **Start** – that's it.

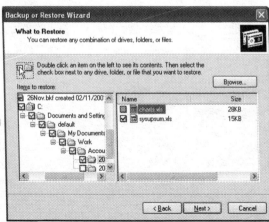

Restoring a file from a backup – not difficult, and far easier than trying to recreate it from scratch!

With any luck you'll never need System Restore, but it's good to know that it is there. Windows XP stores a backup copy of the key system files, known as *system restore points*, at regular intervals. If the files become corrupted, perhaps by 'user error' or when installing software, this will get your PC running again.

1 Go to the **System Tools** menu and select **System Restore**.

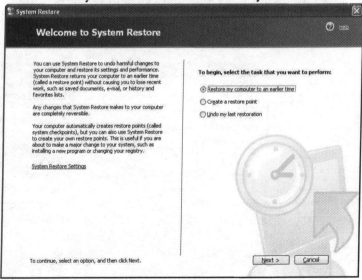

System Restore

Welcome to System Restore   ? Help

You can use System Restore to undo harmful changes to your computer and restore its settings and performance. System Restore returns your computer to an earlier time (called a restore point) without causing you to lose recent work, such as saved documents, e-mail, or history and favorites lists.

Any changes that System Restore makes to your computer are completely reversible.

Your computer automatically creates restore points (called system checkpoints), but you can also use System Restore to create your own restore points. This is useful if you are about to make a major change to your system, such as installing a new program or changing your registry.

System Restore Settings

To begin, select the task that you want to perform:

◉ Restore my computer to an earlier time

○ Create a restore point

○ Undo my last restoration

To continue, select an option, and then click Next.   Next >   Cancel

2 At the first stage, select **Restore my computer…**

3 At the next panel, pick the most recent checkpoint when you
   know that the system was running properly, and click **Next**.

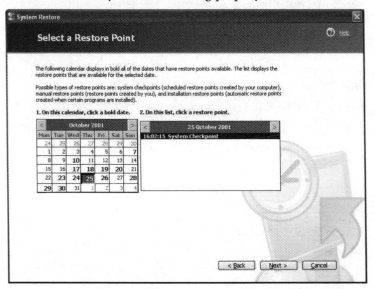

4 You will be prompted to shut down any programs and save
   any open files before setting the operation running. System
   Restore is irreversible. Only run it if you need to!

Create a restore point

A Windows XP computer is robust; modern software and hardware is normally reliable and thoroughly tested, but things do go wrong. Before you do anything which might upset the system, such as installing new kit or making any other major changes, you should create a restore point. This will ensure that there is a current copy of the system files – it may have been a few days since the last system restore point was created.

1 Start **System Restore** and select **Create a restore point**.

2 Type in a description to help you identify it – the point will have the date and time added, so this is not too crucial.

3 Click **Next** to start the process.

tip

It takes only a few minutes to create a restore point and it could save you endless hours of pain!

Format a floppy disk

These are mainly used for backups and for copying files from one PC to another. Before use they must be formatted – this creates a structure on the magnetic surface of the disk, marking it off into storage areas. New disks can be bought ready-formatted. If not, you will have to format them. It only takes a few moments.

1 Place an unformatted disk in the floppy drive.

2 Right-click on the **A:** icon in My Computer and select **Format...** from the menu.

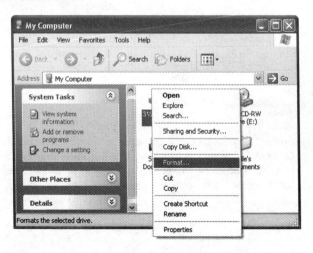

MANAGING YOUR PC

3 At the **Format** dialog box, in **Format Type**, select *Full*.

4 Type a **Label** if wanted – the paper label is more use for identifying floppies.

5 Click **Start**.

Format 3½ Floppy (A:)   ? ×

Capacity:

3.5", 1.44MB, 512 bytes/sector

File system

FAT

Allocation unit size

Default allocation size

Volume label

Format options

☐ Quick Format
☐ Enable Compression
☐ Create an MS-DOS startup disk

Start   Close

A **Quick format** will erase files from a formatted disk – if there are lots of small files, this will be quicker than deleting them

tip

Formatting destroys all the data on a disk. **Do not format the C: drive!** The option is there, but it should only be used as a last-ditch attempt to recover something from the ruins of a total failure – and only ever with professional advice.

Networking

Set up a home network

Setting up even a small network used to be a real chore, but the Home Networking Wizard has transformed the business. It is so easy to use – with two provisos.

- Networking is quite straightforward as long as you are just connecting Windows XP PCs together. You can also connect to PC running earlier versions of Windows, but not as reliably and you won't get the full range of facilities through the link. If you want to share an Internet connection, the PC with the modem must be an XP PC.

- You still have to open the PCs' boxes and install the network cards, and their software, then cable them together. This is not difficult. If you can use a screwdriver, hammer in cable clips (or secure the cable in some other way) and follow instructions, you should be able to set up your network hardware.

The Wizard must be run on each PC. They can be set up, individually, at any time, but it's probably simplest to do all the PCs in one session.

Set up network hardware

There are so many variations here that it is not possible to give any detail of how to do it – the hardware should, in any case, come with detailed instructions for its installation. What follows is just general guidance. You need to understand a little about networking, then look at the PCs and their locations, before going to your dealer to see what they can supply to meet your requirements.

In a typical small network, each PC has a network adapter card, and the PCs are joined by thin coaxial cable. To set this up, each PC must have at least one empty expansion slot.

♦ There are two varieties of expansion slots – PCI and ISA. Older PCs have ISA slots; newer ones have PCI or a mixture of both. Check your PC's documentation to see what it has, then open the case to see if any are empty. Adapter cards also come in PCI and ISA varieties and must match the slots, though you can have PCI cards in some computers and ISA cards in others.

If you do not have empty slots, there are networking systems which work through the USB ports.

You will need one length of cable between each pair of PCs. Any computer dealer should be able to supply you with cables with

their connectors fitted and in suitable lengths. (Measure along
the actual cable run – not the direct distance – between each pair
of PCs. If the dealer does not make up cable to order, then longer
is OK – the spare can be coiled out of the way.) The cable should
be fitted securely, so that it can't be trodden on or tripped over.

+ If there is no convenient, safe or visually acceptable way – you
  do not want cable looped across the living room ceiling – to
  run cable between your PCs, it is possible to connect through
  the electrical mains circuits. (A method which is safer and
  more practical than it sounds at first, but do get the proper
  equipment and consult an expert before embarking on this!)

Network adapters and cables are designed to work at a range of
speeds. If you are mainly using the network to share access to the
modem and a printer, then a basic 10Mb network will do the
job. If it is going to be used for playing high-speed networked
games, you may want something faster.

Once you have a clear idea of what sort of network can be
installed on your system, and what you want to use it for, go to
your local dealer and talk to their network specialist.

Run the Network Setup Wizard

The Wizard handles all the details of setting up the networking software. You just need to tell it a little about your system, and decide the PCs' names and which folders and printers to share. Initially only the *Shared Documents* folder in each PC will be shared across the nework; other can be shared later (page 192).

1 To start the Network Setup Wizard, select the *Set up a network* option in the **New Connection Wizard** or in the **Network Connections** folder.

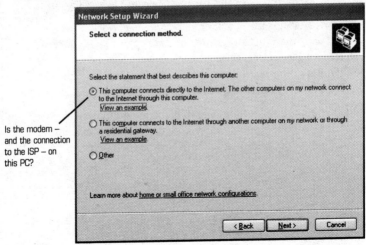

Is the modem – and the connection to the ISP – on this PC?

2 At the Internet Connection stage, tell it if you want to use the Internet from that PC and whether it is has the connection.

3 On the PC with the modem, select *Yes* to let the networked computers use it.

4 Give a name for the computer, and a description if that is needed to help identify it.

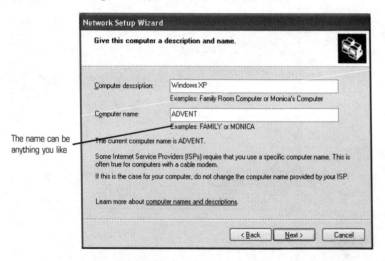

The name can be anything you like

5 Enter a name for the workgroup. The names are entirely up to
   you, but should be single words, and keeping them simple
   and easy to remember is always a good idea. In a home or
   small office, all PCs would normally be in the same
   workgroup.

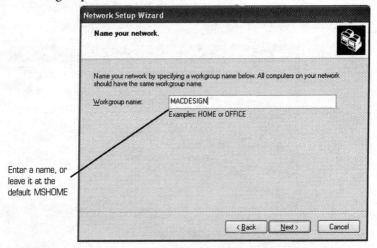

Enter a name, or
leave it at the
default MSHOME

tip

Once the network is in place, you can fine-tune the access to
the folders and printers (see *Share resources*, page 192).

6 You will be shown a summary of the settings. Check them, and if everything seems OK, click **Next**.

7 At the final stage you will be offered the chance to create a special **Network Setup disk** to use on any non-XP PCs that you might want to link onto the network.

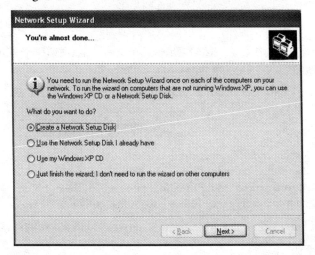

* The PC must be restarted afterwards for the network settings to take effect.

Share resources

You can change the level of access that other users have to the folders and printers on a PC at any time. These changes take effect immediately.

A folder can be shared in two ways:

* *Read-only* will allow other users to read the files or run the programs that are stored there, but it will not let them edit or delete files, or store new files.

* *Full access* allows other users to treat the folder as if it were on their own PC.

At either level, access can be controlled by a password.

If you share a drive, all its folders are initially shared in the same way. You can then adjust the share level on individual folders, but this can only be to give *greater* access – not *less*. If a disk is shared at full access, then every folder within it is fully shared.

* If you only want others to have access to selected folders, set the disk to **Not Shared**.

Share a printer

1 Open the **Printers** folder from the **Start** menu.

2 Right-click on the printer and select **Sharing...**

3 Turn sharing on/off and type a name.

4 Click **OK**.

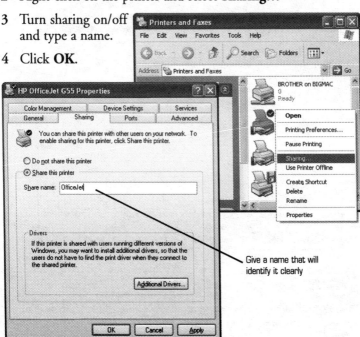

Give a name that will identify it clearly

Share folders

1 Run Windows Explorer or My Computer.

2 Right-click on the folder and select **Sharing and Security…**

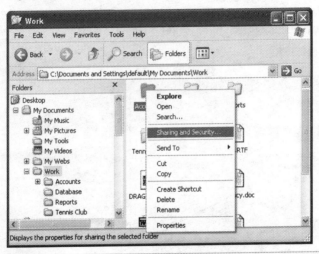

tip

When you share a disk or folder, every folder within it is also shared at the same level of access.

3 Tick **Share this folder on the network** and enter a share
   name.

4 If you want others to have full access to the folder, tick **Allow
   network users to change my files**.

5 Click **OK**.

You can share a folder with other
users on the same PC, without
opening it to remote network users

Clear this box if you only
want to give other users
read permission

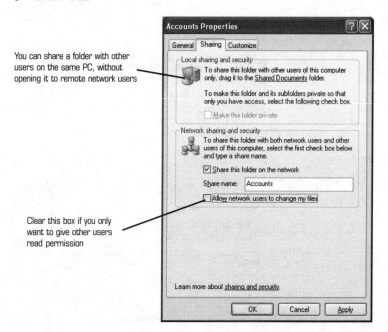

Explore My Network Places

Once the network is set up, use **My Network Places** to view the other PCs' shared drives – it works just like My Computer.

1 Open **My Network Places** from the Desktop.

2 Click on a folder to open it.

3 Open files as normal.

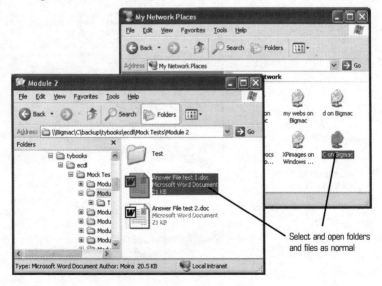

Select and open folders and files as normal

Use applications on the network

New Windows software can handle network connections with no trouble. When you want to open or save a file, it will let you reach across the network and link to any shared folder. Older applications were often not designed for use on networks, and will only allow you to reach files on drives on the same PC. Windows XP has a neat solution. You can *map* networked drives – assign drive letters to them. The C: drive on the PC in the study, for example, which might have a network name of //Study/ C/ could then be referred to as F:/ by the PC in the living room.

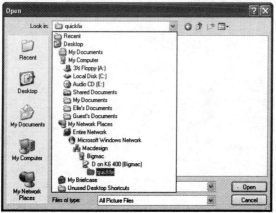

In the new Open and Save dialog boxes, you can reach the network through the **Look in** folder display

Map drives

A drive is mapped once, at the start of a session, from Windows Explorer or My Computer and can then be referred to by its assigned letter by any application. A mapped drive can be picked from the **Drives** list in the Open and Save dialog boxes of older Windows applications.

1 Run **Windows Explorer** or **My Computer**.

2 Open the **Tools** menu and select **Map Network Drive…**

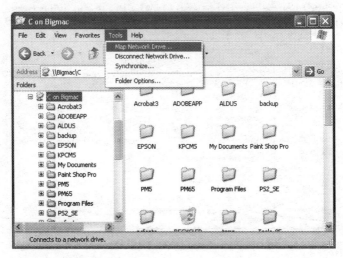

3 At the **Map Network Drive** wizard, select a drive letter – the next free letter, probably E: or F:, is as good as any.

4 Type the path to the folder, if you know it, otherwise, click **Browse...** and select the folder.

5 If you always need to map this drive, tick **Reconnect at logon** to save having to do this again.

6 Click **Finish**.

Map Network Drive

Windows can help you connect to a shared network folder and assign a drive letter to the connection so that you can access the folder using My Computer.

Specify the drive letter for the connection and the folder that you want to connect to:

Drive: F:

Folder: \\Bigmac\C   Browse...

Example: \\server\share

☑ Reconnect at logon

Connect using a different user name.

Sign up for online storage or connect to a network server.

< Back   Finish   Cancel

Map the drive every time?

Browse For Folder

Select a shared network folder

- My Network Places
  - Entire Network
    - Microsoft Terminal Services
    - Microsoft Windows Network
      - Macdesign
    - Web Client Network
  - Accounts on Windows XP (Advent)
  - C on Bigmac
    - Acrobat3
    - ADOBEAPP

Make New Folder   OK   Cancel

It's much easier to browse for a folder than to type its path yourself!

ACCESSORIES

Text and images

Discover WordPad

Don't underrate WordPad just because it's free. It's fine for writing letters, essays, reports and anything else where you want to be able to edit text efficiently, formatting it with fonts, styles and colours, and perhaps incorporating graphics or other files.

- When entering text, just keep typing when you reach the edge of the page – the text will be wrapped round to the next line. Only press the **Enter** key at the end of a paragraph.

- Most formatting can be done through the toolbar. Select the text, then pick a font or size from the drop-down lists, or click the B bold, I italic, U underline, or other buttons.

- The ≡ left, ≡ centre and ≡ right alignment buttons determine how the text lines up with the edges of the paper.

tip

The techniques you learn with WordPad can be applied to Word and most other word-processors.

- The 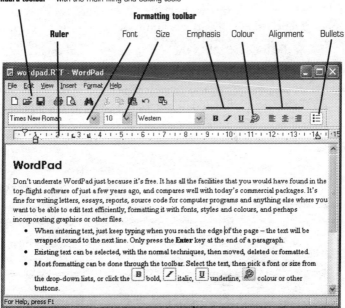 bullets button indents text from the left, with a blob at the start of each paragraph.

- Alignment and bullet formats apply to whole paragraphs. A paragraph is selected if the cursor is within it, or if any part of the paragraph is selected.

Standard toolbar – with the main filing and editing tools

Formatting toolbar

Ruler Font Size Emphasis Colour Alignment Bullets

WordPad

Don't underrate WordPad just because it's free. It has all the facilities that you would have found in the top-flight software of just a few years ago, and compares well with today's commercial packages. It's fine for writing letters, essays, reports, source code for computer programs and anything else where you want to be able to edit text efficiently, formatting it with fonts, styles and colours, and perhaps incorporating graphics or other files.

- When entering text, just keep typing when you reach the edge of the page – the text will be wrapped round to the next line. Only press the **Enter** key at the end of a paragraph.

- Existing text can be selected, with the normal techniques, then moved, deleted or formatted.

- Most formatting can be done through the toolbar. Select the text, then pick a font or size from the drop-down lists, or click the B bold, / italic, U underline, colour or other buttons.

Set indents and tabs

Indents push the text in from the page margins. The first line of a paragraph can be – and often is – indented less or more than later lines. Use the **First line indent** to set the first line and the **Left indent** to set depth of the indent for the rest of the paragraph.

Tabs are used to line up text in columns. In WordPad there are only *left* tabs – these align the columns of text by their left sides.

* To set the indents, select the text to be indented then drag their markers as required.

* To set tabs, select the text to which they will apply then click on the ruler to create a new tab, or drag an existing one to a new place.

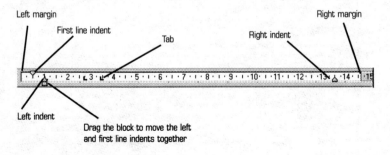

Left margin

First line indent

Tab

Right indent

Right margin

· 1 · 1 · 2 · 3 · 4 · 5 · 1 · 6 · 1 · 7 · 1 · 8 · 1 · 9 · 1 · 10 · 1 · 11 · 1 · 12 · 1 · 13 · 14 · 1 · 15

Left indent

Drag the block to move the left and first line indents together

Format fonts

You can set most font options from the toolbar buttons, but you get better control through the **Font** dialog box. Here you can set all aspects of a font, and preview the effects of your choices.

1 Select the text to be formatted.

2 Open the dialog box with **Format ➤ Font**.

3 Work through the options to define the font – watch the **Sample** text as you change the settings.

4 Click **OK**.

You will find similar panels in all applications that use fonts

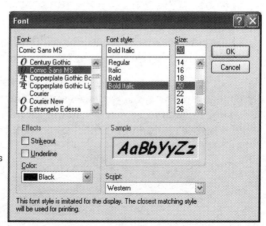

Define the Page Setup

The **Page Setup** panel, opened from the **File** menu option, controls the basic size and layout of the page – for all pages in the document.

* The **Paper Size** and **Source** settings rarely need changing – if you've set your printer properties correctly. If you are printing on card or special paper, change the **Source** to *Manual*, if the option is available.

* In the **Orientation** area, *Portrait* is the normal way up; use *Landscape* if you want to print with the paper sideways.

* The **Margins** set the overall limits to the printable area. You can use the indents to reduce the width of text within the margins, but you cannot extend out beyond them.

* Click the **Printer** button to reach its **Properties** panel to change any settings at that level – you might, for example, want to switch to a lower resolution for printing a draft copy, or a higher resolution for the final output. (See pages 152 to 165 for more on printers.)

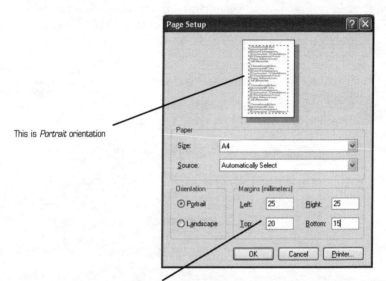

This is *Portrait* orientation

Measurements here are in millimetres,
but can be changed on the **Options** panel
that opens from the **View** menu

Insert graphics and other objects

WordPad is not limited to text only. Pictures, graphs, spreadsheets, audio and video clips – in fact just about any object that can be produced by any Windows application – can be incorporated into a WordPad document. The technique is much the same for any object.

1 Open the **Insert** menu and select **Object...**

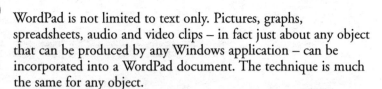

2 If the object does not yet exist, select **Create New** and pick the **Object Type**, then click **OK**.

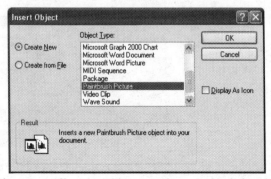

The application will open. When you have created the object, save it if you want to keep a copy for future use, then select the new **Exit & Return to Document** option from its **File** menu.

3 If you want to use an existing object, select **Create from File**, and browse through your folders to locate it.

4 Back in WordPad, you can resize the object if necessary.

The position of the object across the page can be set using the alignment buttons

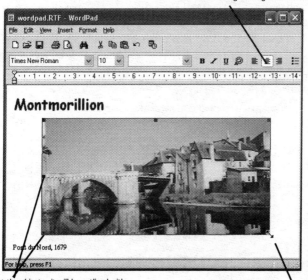

Select the object – it will be outlined with handles at the corners and mid-edges

Point to a handle to get the double-headed arrow then drag in or out as required

ADJUSTING THE SIZE OF AN IMAGE IN WORDPAD. AN INSERTED OBJECT CAN BE EDITED BY DOUBLE-CLICKING ON IT – THIS OPENS THE SOURCE APPLICATION. USE EXIT & RETURN WHEN YOU HAVE FINISHED EDITING

Preview before printing

Most applications have a Print Preview facility, and it is always useful, as it can be difficult to tell how a document will look on paper. Use the Preview to get a better idea of the final output, before you print. Do the images and headings have the impact that you want? Do you get bad breaks in the text at the ends of pages? If it looks good, you can print from here by clicking **Print**, if not, click **Close** to return to WordPad for that final tweaking.

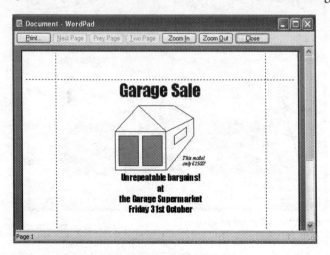

USE THE PRINT PREVIEW TO CHECK THE LAYOUT. YOU CAN PRINT FROM HERE, OR CLOSE TO RETURN TO EDITING

Save a file

In all applications you should save early and save often! Don't wait until you have finished writing that eight-page report before you save it. Applications can crash, hardware can fail, plugs get knocked out and we all make mistakes! The first save may take a few moments, but later saves are done at the click of a button.

To save a file for the first time:

1 Open the **File** menu and select **Save As...**

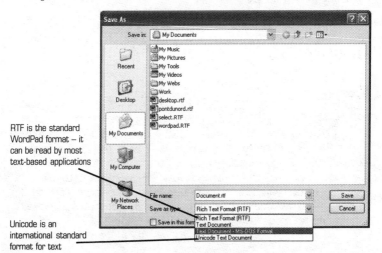

RTF is the standard WordPad format – it can be read by most text-based applications

Unicode is an international standard format for text

2   At the dialog box, select the folder.

3   Change the default *Document* in the filename to something that will remind you what it is about.

4   If you want to save in a different format, pick one from the **Save as type** drop-down list.

5   Click **Save**.

To resave the current document:

♦   Click 🖫 – that's it!

When you close the document, or exit from WordPad, if you have not saved the document in its final state, you will be prompted to do so.

---

tip

If you use WordPad to create HTML documents (Web pages) or the source code for programs, you'll save the file as Text. WordPad will automatically add *.txt* to the end of the filename – which is not wanted! For example, the Web page that you wanted to call *mypage.htm* will be saved as *mypage.htm.txt*. After you exit WordPad, find the file in My Computer and edit the filename to get rid of the extra extension.

Open a file

Next time that you want to work on the document, open it from the **File** menu. Either:

- Select **Open** and then browse for the file – the dialog box is used in almost exactly the same way as the **Save** dialog box.

- Or if it is one of the files that you have used recently, it will be listed at the bottom of the **File** menu. Select it from here.

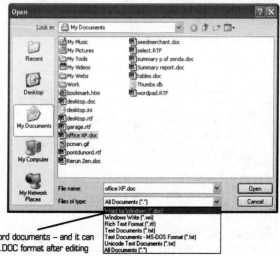

WordPad can read Word documents – and it can then resave the file in .DOC format after editing

Use Notepad

This is a text editor, not a word-processor. Text can be typed and edited just as it can in WordPad, but it cannot be formatted. Because it is such a simple program, it starts up faster and uses less memory than any word-processor. It is good for producing plain text files – such as memos, program code and text which is to be handed on to someone else for formatting.

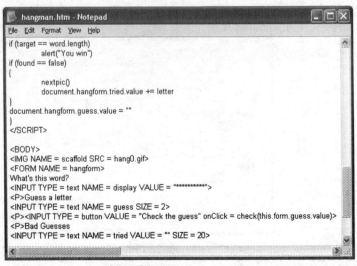

```
hangman.htm - Notepad
File  Edit  Format  View  Help

if (target == word.length)
          alert("You win")
if (found == false)
{
          nextpic()
          document.hangform.tried.value += letter
}
document.hangform.guess.value = ""
}
</SCRIPT>

<BODY>
<IMG NAME = scaffold SRC = hang0.gif>
<FORM NAME = hangform>
What's this word?
<INPUT TYPE = text NAME = display VALUE = "**********">
<P>Guess a letter
<INPUT TYPE = text NAME = guess SIZE = 2>
<P><INPUT TYPE = button VALUE = "Check the guess" onClick = check(this.form.guess.value)>
<P>Bad Guesses
<INPUT TYPE = text NAME = tried VALUE = "" SIZE = 20>
```

EDITING A PROGRAM IN NOTEPAD. YOU CAN SET THE FONT, BUT ONLY FOR THE SCREEN DISPLAY OF ALL THE TEXT.

Apart from the normal File and Edit commands, the only significant facility offered by Notepad is a search routine – useful in programming for tracking down variables.

Edit → Find... opens the **Find** panel, where you can specify what to look for.

Edit → Find Next simply repeats the last search.

Use the Character Map

You will find **Character Map** on the **System Tools** menu – don't ask me why! It's a useful tool and one that I like to have close to hand. It allows you to see the characters available in any font, and to copy individual characters from there into a document.

Next time that you want a symbol, accented letter or other unusual character in any document, use the Map.

1   From the **Start** menu, go to the **Programs → Accessories → System Tools** menu and select the **Character Map**.

2   Pick a font from the drop-down list – Symbol, Webdings and Wingdings are the main fonts for decorative characters, and you will find foreign letters and mathematical symbols in most other fonts.

3   Click on a character or hold down the left button and move across the display – the character under the cursor will be enlarged.

4   To copy characters into a document, click **Select** – the current one will be added to the **Characters to copy** set – then click **Copy** when you have all you want. Return to your document and use **Edit → Paste**. The character(s) will be copied in, formatted to the chosen font.

Click for an enlargement

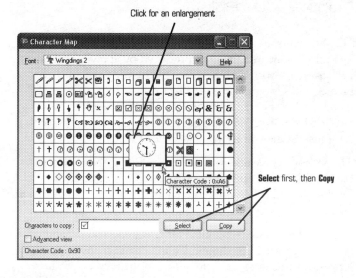

TEXT AND IMAGES

Select first, then Copy

tip
Remember that the appearance of the character is largely determined by the font.

Dabble with Paint

Graphics software falls into two broad groups. With some, including **Paint**, the image is produced by applying colour to a background – with each new line overwriting anything that may be beneath. Using these is very like real painting. You may be able to wipe out a mistake while the paint is still wet, but as soon as it has dried it is fixed on the canvas. (Paint allows you to undo the last move; some will let you backtrack further.)

The second type works with objects – lines, circles, text notes, etc. – that remain separate, and can be moved, deleted, recoloured and otherwise changed at any point. Word's drawing facility works this way.

I use Paint regularly – it's ideal for trimming and tidying screenshots for books, though I don't expect many of you will want it for this purpose. Though it can be used to produce intricate images, these require a great deal of time and skill – and can be created more successfully on a computer art package, with a full set of shading, shaping and manipulating tools. Paint is probably best used to draw simple diagrams, or to get an idea of how this type of graphics software works.

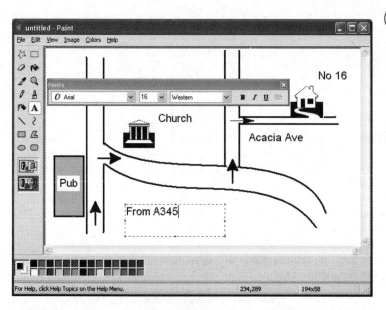

USING PAINT TO CREATE A DIAGRAM. THE TEXT TOOLBAR GIVES YOU THE FULL RANGE OF FONTS AND THE MAIN STYLE EFFECTS

The Toolbox

There is a simple but adequate set of tools.

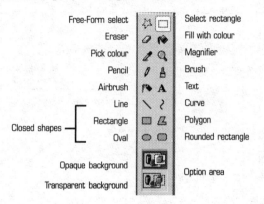

A little experimentation will show how they all work, but note these points:

* The *Pencil, Brush* and *Airbrush* lay down the foreground colour when the left button is held down, and the background colour when the right button is pressed.

* With the *Line* and the closed shapes, click where you want one end of the line or corner of the shape to be, then drag to the opposite end/corner.

- *Pick colour* is used to select a colour off the screen – press the right button to use it to select a background colour.

- If you hold down the right button when using the *Eraser*, it will replace anything in the foreground colour with the background colour, without affecting anything else.

Most of the tools have options that can be set in the area below the toolbar.

- When you select an area (or paste an image from a file or from the Clipboard) the background can be transparent or opaque.

- You can set the size of the *Eraser, Brush, Airbrush, Line* and *Curve*. N.B. the Line thickness applies to the closed shapes.

- The *Magnifier* is 4× by default, but can be 2×, 6× or 8×.

- The *Pencil* is only ever 1 pixel wide.

- *Closed shapes* can be outline or fill only, or both.

Work with selected areas

The rectangular and free-form selectors can be used to select an area of the screen.

1   To select a regular area, use the *Rectangle select* tool. Click at the top left of the area and drag to the opposite corner – a dashed frame indicates the area being selected.

2   To select an irregular area, use the *Freeform select* tool. Drag an outline around the area – it'll probably be wobbly, but as long as it selects the right bit, why worry?

3   Once selected, an area can be:

*   *Deleted* – which can be a neater way to remove excess bits than using the eraser.

*   *Copied* – handy for creating repeating patterns.

*   *Saved as a file* – use **Edit ➜ Copy To...** and give a filename.

*   *Dragged elsewhere* on screen.

*   *Flipped* (mirrored) horizontally or vertically, or rotated in 90° increments – use **Image ➜ Flip/Rotate** for these effects.

*   *Stretched* – to enlarge, shrink or distort; or *skewed*, either horizontally or vertically – use **Image ➜ Stretch/Skew**.

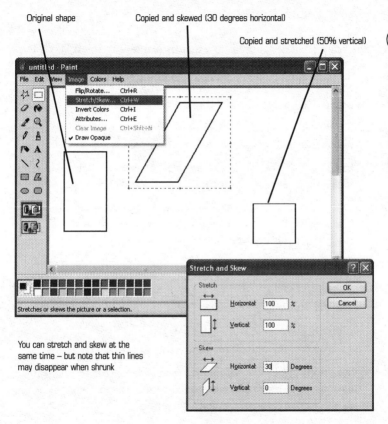

Original shape

Copied and skewed (30 degrees horizontal)

Copied and stretched (50% vertical)

You can stretch and skew at the same time – but note that thin lines may disappear when shrunk

Select and mix colours

The colour palette is used in much the same way in all Windows programs. You can select a colour – use the left button for the foreground and the right for the background – or mix your own.

To define a colour:

1 Double-click on a colour in the **Color Box** or use **Colors →
   Edit Colors** to open the **Edit Colors** panel.

2 Initially only the **Basic colors** will be visible. Click **Define
   Custom Colors** to open the full panel.

3 Drag the cross-hair cursor in the main square to set the Red/
   Green/Blue balance, and move the arrow up or down the left
   scale to set the light/dark level.

4 Colours can also be set by typing in values, but note that you
   are mixing light, not paint.

   ◆ Red and green make yellow;

   ◆ Red, green and blue make grey/white;

   ◆ The more you use, the lighter the colour.

5 When you have the colour you want, click **Add to Custom
   Colors**. The new colour will replace the one currently selected
   in the Color Box on the main screen.

Set the Red/Green/Blue balance

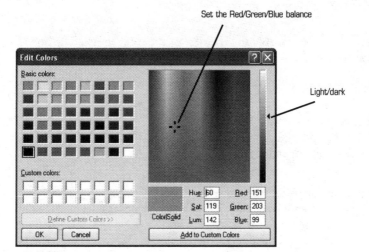

Light/dark

Draw a curve in Paint

The *Curve* is probably the trickiest of the tools to use. The line can have one or two curves to it.

1 Draw a line between the points where the curve will start and end.

2 Drag to create the first curve – exaggerate the curve as it will normally be reduced at the next stage.

3 If the line is to have a second curve, drag it out now – as long as the mouse button is down, the line will flex to follow the cursor.

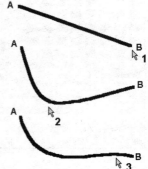

or

4 For a simple curve, just click at the end of the line.

---

tip

If you go wrong any time – and you will with the Curve – use **Edit → Undo**. This removes the effect of the last action.

Save or open a picture file

A normal **Save** will save the whole working area, in 24-bit (high colour) bitmap format. These are large files. Files will be smaller if you use the more efficient JPEG format, or if you save with fewer colours as BMP or (256 colour) GIFs.

◆ You can also use **Edit → Copy To...** to save a selected part of an image as a separate file.

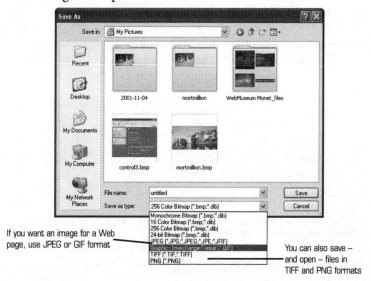

If you want an image for a Web page, use JPEG or GIF format

You can also save – and open – files in TIFF and PNG formats

Scan images into files

The **Scanner and Camera Wizard** gives you a neat way take
images in from a scanner or a digital camera, and store them in a
folder.

The wizard first calls up the scanner's control panel. Here you can
define the picture type and the area to be scanned – use the
preview to define the area, unless you want to scan a full page. At
the next stage, you specify the file's name, its format and the
folder in which to store it. After the picture has been captured,
you will be given the option of also publishing the images on
your Web site or ordering printed copies from an online photo
printers.

If you want to take an image directly into a graphics program,
for editing, then it is normally simpler to start from within
that program – look for **From Scanner or Camera** or **Acquire
Image** or similar command on the **File** menu.

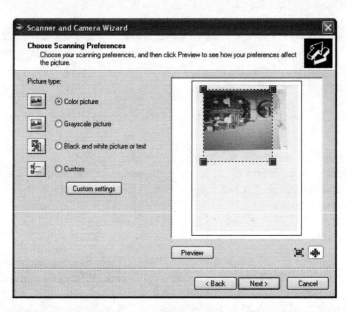

A SCANNER CONTROL PANEL – YOU WILL SEE THE SAME PANEL YOU START YOUR SCANNER FROM WITH PAINT OR OTHER GRAPHICS SOFTWARE. IF YOU ARE DOING A HIGH RESOLUTION SCAN, DEFINE THE AREA TIGHTLY TO KEEP THE FILE SIZE AND SCANNING TIME DOWN AS FAR AS POSSIBLE.

Utilities and media

Calculator

Pack away that pocket calculator. You don't need it on your desk now that you have one on your Desktop!

The Calculator can work in two modes – Standard or Scientific. In either case, you use it in the same way that you would a hand-held calculator. Enter the numbers, arithmetic operators and functions either by clicking on the screen keys, or by using your keyboard. (If you want to use the keyboard in the Scientific mode, look in the Help file for the keyboard equivalents.)

It has the same limitations as a simple pocket calculator – you can only store one value in memory at a time (**MS** to store it, **M+** to add to the value in memory, **MR** to recall it and **MC** to clear it); and you cannot print your results. If you want more than this, use a spreadsheet!

Media Player

Media Player is a multi-purpose audio/video player. It can handle sound files in MIDI and in the native Windows format, WAVE, audio CDs, and video in the Video for Windows (AVI), Media Audio/Video (WMA and ASF) or ActiveMovie formats.

Video

Newer, faster hardware and more efficient software have significantly improved the quality of videos on PC, but they are still grainy and jerky. The main sources of videos are multimedia packages, demos and samples on CDs, and the Internet.

There are three main ways to get video from the Internet:

- Clips for downloading – the new high-compression formats have brought a better balance between download time and playing time. 1Mb of video gives you around 90 seconds of playing time, and will take up to 10 minutes to download.

- *Streaming* video in TV and webcam broadcasts and in movie and pop video clips. Here the videos are played as they download. The images are jerkier, but at least you don't have to wait to see whether they are worth watching at all.

- **Home movies e-mailed to you by relatives, who have been playing with Movie Maker (see page 239).**

Play a CD

Want some music while you work? Let Media Player play a CD for you.

1 Load in the CD and wait for Media Player to start and to read in the track information.

◆ The CD will play in the tracks in their playlist sequence – initially this will be the standard order.

2 To change the order of tracks, click on one to select it, then drag up or down.

3 To skip over tracks, select them, then right-click and choose **Disable** from the shortcut menu.

It's worth taking time over organizing the playlist, as the information that you enter is stored in a file on the hard disk and will be reused next time the same CD is loaded.

tip

Media Player may struggle with the last tracks on long CDs.

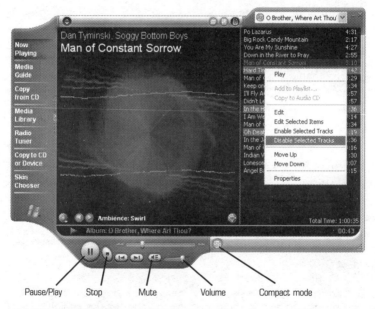

MEDIA PLAYER, SHOWING THE PLAYLIST FOR AN AUDIO CD

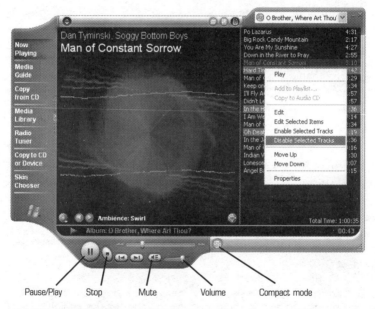

Pause/Play   Stop   Mute   Volume   Compact mode

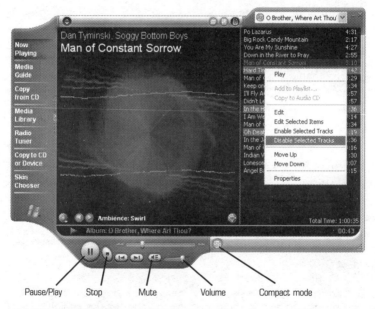

Listen to the radio

The **Radio Tuner** offers another way to get to the same Internet radio stations that you can reach through the Radio toolbar in Internet Explorer.

1 Go online.

2 Open **Media Player** and click the **Radio Tuner** button.

3 Media Player will link to **media.com**. On the left, you will see a list of a dozen pre-set stations, catering to a range of tastes – pick a station, or…

4 Browse for a new station. You can either work through the whole – enormous – list, or start by picking a format, and choosing a station from a more specialised list.

5 Internet Explorer will normally open to show you the station's Web site. This can be closed down if not wanted, to save screen space and speed up download of the broadcast.

tip

Obviously, if you are paying for your phone time when you are online, this is not an efficient way to listen to the radio!

The reception is not brilliant – expect some gaps and crackles – but can you
pick up stations in the USA, Australia, Italy, Vietnam, etc. on your Hi Fi?

LISTENING TO JAZZ FM, WHILE LOOKING TO SEE WHAT STATIONS OFFER CLASSICAL MUSIC – THERE ARE DOZENS.
HOW DO I CHOOSE ONE?!

Choose a skin

Once the playlist is set up and the
CD is playing, you can switch
into compact mode. This doesn't
just occupy less screen space; it also
has some great 'skins', which vary
from the sublime to the ridicu-
lous (I like this one, it's silly!)

To choose and use a skin:

1   Click the **Skin Chooser** button.

2   Click on a skin in the list and click **Apply Skin**.

3   To restore the full display, click 🔲 – this is hard to spot on
    some skins.

If a skin has a screen, a 'visualization' will run in it while music is
playing. If you want to change this, open the **View** menu, point
to **Visualization**, select a set then pick one from there. None seem
to respond much to changes in rhythm, pitch or volume, so don't
expect a *son et lumière* experience.

Links to Microsoft's Web site where you
will find more skins to choose from

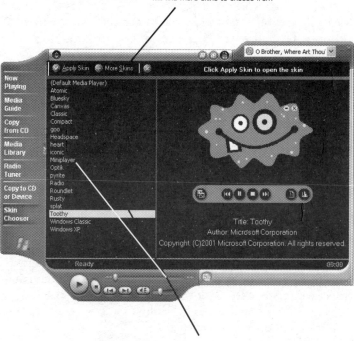

A skin is a more compact display than the full player – and if
compactness is the main reason for using a skin, choose *Miniplayer*

Manage your music

Media Player's other tabs allow you to manage your music (and video) in different ways.

Media Guide

This links to Microsoft's Media Guide site, from where you can download samples, clips and much more. Have a browse next time you are online.

Media Library

Use this to organize the audio and video files currently on your PC. You can list audio files by album, artist or genre, and video files by author. Having located a file, double-click on it to run it.

Copy to CD or Device

If you own a pocket or palm-size PC, you can use this facility to copy files from your hard drive, or from an audio CD onto the device.

Movie Maker

You can use this to edit digital video, taking images in directly from your camera. The video is automatically split into clips, which can then be split further or trimmed and set into a new sequence. You can merge in other video clips, or add still images, for titles and credits, or a voice-over or background music. Altogether, this is quite a competent editing suite. If you have the time and the skill, you can produce some good movies.

The Movie Maker format takes around 10Kb for each second of playing time. This means that video files are not small, though they are very much more compact than the ones produced by older formats, and sharing them with distant friends and relatives via the Internet is now quite feasible.

There are two ways to do it:

* Send the movie by e-mail. Files are increased in size by 50% when attached to a message (it's to do with the way that data is transferred through the mail system), but you can normally download e-mail at 3Kb or more per second.

* Upload the file to your home page, and just send the URL to people. There are two catches to this: you have to have at least a basic grasp of putting home pages together, and download times from the Web are typically less than 2Kb per second.

What it boils down to is that it is going to take your friends and
relatives around one minute to download 100Kb of video, which
will play for 10 seconds. That 10-minute video of the little one's
birthday party will take over an hour to get, but if they are on the
other side of the world, it may be an hour well spent.

The clips can be trimmed and rearranged freely

PLAYING WITH THE SAMPLE FILE IN MOVIE MAKER. I DON'T THINK I'VE GOT A FUTURE IN MOVIES – YOU MAY HAVE!

Notes

Notes

Notes